Mr Herbert P. Hughes

CAMBRIDGE BOOK OF
ENGLISH VERSE
1900–39

CAMBRIDGE
BOOK OF
ENGLISH VERSE
1900-39

Edited by
ALLEN FREER
and
JOHN ANDREW

CAMBRIDGE
at the University Press
1971

Published by the Syndics of the Cambridge University Press
Bentley House, 200 Euston Road, London NW1 2DB
American Branch: 32 East 57th Street, New York, N.Y.10022

ISBN
0 521 07763 X clothbound
0 521 09625 1 paperback

First published 1970
Reprinted 1971

Printed in Great Britain
at the University Printing House, Cambridge
(Brooke Crutchley, University Printer)

CONTENTS

[v]

CONTENTS

viii   *CONTENTS*

PREFACE

We have prepared this anthology in the hope that it will be attractive to the general reader, and of use in the upper forms of schools, and to students—including foreign students—studying English poetry in the twentieth century. Our aim was to prepare a selection of verse which should do justice to those who seem to us to be the most significant poets of the first forty years of the century and, at the same time, to ensure that they were represented by poems which were not only typical of their interests, perceptions, and method but also were good poetry in themselves. In brief, we wanted an anthology which contained no dross but which would give a reasonable account of the development of English poetry before the Second World War, as seen in the work of the most important poets. This meant deciding who the most important poets are, but we believe that our judgement will be accepted by most readers, who will also accept the apparent anomaly of our including Hopkins and some early Hardy. We should have liked to include more of Eliot's work, but were restricted in our choice by the policy towards anthologies of his publishers.

We had then to decide whether to annotate the poems or not. Some friends, teachers for the most part, advised us against annotation because they found it irritating when anthologizers tried to do the teacher's work for him. Against that advice, we had to accept the view that the general reader and the foreign student would, perhaps, welcome some notes, not because they would necessarily give a 'true' reading of the poem but because they might at least indicate the way in which the poem might be approached, and would help with those difficulties which still, in spite of the passage of time, remain, and hinder understanding. Whether the notes are useful or not we now leave to the reader to decide. We, for our part, have learnt a great deal in trying to provide them and we stand indebted to the many critics whose books we have mentioned in our lists of suggested reading for the particular and general insights that we have gained from them. There is always something arbitrary about an anthology and we cannot hope that our choice will be acceptable to all those who take up this book. But if we have succeeded in giving some idea of the variety of achievement to be found in the work of these poets, then we shall have achieved the modest end we set ourselves.

A.F.
J.M.Y.A.

ACKNOWLEDGEMENTS

Thanks are due to the following for permission to quote copyright material.

Chatto and Windus Ltd and the author's Literary Estate for the poems by Isaac Rosenberg, from *The Collected Poems of Isaac Rosenberg*; Chatto and Windus Ltd and Mr Harold Owen for the poems by Wilfred Owen, from *The Collected Poems of Wilfred Owen*, edited by C. Day Lewis; Faber and Faber Ltd for the poems by T. S. Eliot, from *Collected Poems 1909–1962*; for the poems by W. H. Auden, from *Collected Shorter Poems 1927–1957*; and for the poems by Ezra Pound, from *Personae* and from *The Cantos*; Laurence Pollinger Limited and the Estate of the late Mrs Frieda Lawrence for the poems by D. H. Lawrence, from *The Complete Poems of D. H. Lawrence*; The Literary Trustees of Walter de la Mare and The Society of Authors as their representative, for the poems by Walter de la Mare; The Trustees of the Hardy Estate, The Macmillan Company of Canada Ltd and Macmillan and Co. Ltd for the poems by Thomas Hardy, from *The Collected Poems of Thomas Hardy*; Mrs Helen Thomas for the poems by Edward Thomas; M. B. Yeats and Macmillan and Co. Ltd for the poems by W. B. Yeats, from *The Collected Poems of W. B. Yeats*.

GERARD MANLEY HOPKINS

Gerard Manley Hopkins was born on 28 July 1844, at Stratford in Essex. His family was prosperous and cultivated. His father, a Consul-General for Hawaii, wrote a history of Hawaii, several books on his profession and three volumes of verse; he also enjoyed music and delighted in word-play and puns. Other members of the family and relatives had talents in music and drawing. The family were High Anglicans.

The eldest of nine children, Gerard Manley Hopkins was a precocious and exceptionally gifted boy: and at Highgate School he won the school Poetry Prize when he was sixteen. Already his poetic gifts were rapidly developing, along with an unusual ability in painting and drawing. In 1863 he went up to Balliol College, Oxford, to read Classics.

At Oxford Hopkins felt liberated sufficiently to give much time to the study and writing of poetry; to his painting and drawing; and to prove himself in Jowett's estimation to be the best classical scholar of his year. His diaries written at Oxford are full of detailed, accurate notes on nature and architecture, accompanied by exquisite drawings and paintings showing a vivid response to the world around him. Always in these sketches and drafts of poems and notes there is a passionate desire to arrive at the inwardness of the object or the form contemplated, to know and realize afresh in terms of art, its essential nature, its 'self'.

Hopkins' thought and writing was influenced by Walter Pater whose pupil he became. A stronger influence was that of Newman. By upbringing a High Anglican, Hopkins, strongly influenced by the Oxford High Church movement, felt his position as an Anglican to be untenable. In October 1866 he was received by Newman into the Roman Catholic Church, to the great distress of his family. He remained in Oxford for a further year, adding a First in 'Greats' to his First in 'Mods', and then took a teaching post at the Oratory School in Birmingham. In 1868 he resolved to become a priest and a Jesuit. In May of the same year he destroyed his poems.

[1]

For two years he studied at Roehampton and then, after taking his first vows of poverty, chastity and obedience, he went to Stonyhurst to study Philosophy. There followed a further period at Roehampton where Hopkins taught Rhetoric before he went to St Beuno's College in North Wales to study Theology. During these seven years Hopkins wrote no poetry 'except for two or three little presentation pieces which occasion called for'. But in 1875, having read and been deeply moved by an account of the death by drowning of five Franciscan nuns in the shipwreck of the *Deutschland* in the mouth of the Thames, he spoke of this to his rector who said that he wished 'someone would write a poem on the subject'. 'On this hint', writes Hopkins, 'I set to work and, though my hand was out at first, produced one.' The poem that Hopkins produced proved to be one of the greatest religious poems in the language. The Catholic periodical, *The Month*, accepted it, but after a time they withdrew and dared not print it.

On 23 September 1877, Hopkins was ordained priest. The conditions he encountered in parishes in Manchester, Liverpool and Glasgow shocked and appalled him, and his health suffered. It was with relief that he came back to Roehampton for his 'Tertianship' (his third year of probation as a Jesuit). After the vice and horrors he had seen in the northern industrial cities, he welcomed the opportunity for renewal and restoration.

After two years' teaching at Stonyhurst, Hopkins became Professor of Greek and Fellow of the Royal University at University College, Dublin, a post he retained until his death from typhoid fever in 1889, seven weeks before his forty-fifth birthday.

Hopkins entrusted his poems to his friend, Robert Bridges, for safe-keeping until he thought the time opportune for their publication. Judging them to be in advance of their time, Bridges published a few poems in *Poets and Poetry of the Century* (1893), and a further few in his own anthology *The Spirit of Man* (1915). It was not until 1918 that the first full edition of Hopkins' *Poems* was published and, though slow to sell (it was 1928 before the 750 copies of the first edition were sold), Hopkins' reputation has grown steadily with the passing of time.

As a poet, his reputation and his effect belong particularly to the twentieth century. That is why he is included in this anthology.

FURTHER READING

Abbott, Claude C. (ed.). *Correspondence of Gerard Manley Hopkins and R. W. Dixon*. Oxford University Press, 1935.

Abbott, Claude C. (ed.). *Letters of Gerard Manley Hopkins to Robert Bridges*. Oxford University Press, 1935.

House, Humphry (ed., and completed by Graham Storey). *Journals and Papers of Gerard Manley Hopkins*. 2nd ed., revised and enlarged, Oxford University Press, 1959.

CRITICAL WORKS

Gardner, W. H. *Gerard Manley Hopkins: a Study of Poetic Idiosyncrasy in Relation to Poetic Tradition*. 2 vols., revised ed., Secker and Warburg, 1959.

Leavis, F. R. *New Bearings in English Poetry*. 2nd ed., Chatto and Windus, 1950.

Lees, F. N. 'Gerard Manley Hopkins' in vol. 6 of *The Pelican Guide to English Literature*, ed. Boris Ford. Revised ed., Penguin Books, 1964.

Weyand, Norman, S.J. (ed.). *Immortal Diamond: Studies in Gerard Manley Hopkins*. Sheed and Ward, 1949.

Winter with the Gulf Stream

The boughs, the boughs are bare enough
But earth has never felt the snow.
Frost-furred our ivies are and rough

With bills of rime the brambles shew.
The hoarse leaves crawl on hissing ground   5
Because the sighing wind is low.

But if the rain-blasts be unbound
And from dank feathers wring the drops
The clogged brook runs with choking sound

Kneading the mounded mire that stops   10
His channel under clammy coats
Of foliage fallen in the copse.

A simple passage of weak notes
Is all the winter bird dare try.
The bugle moon by daylight floats   15

So glassy white about the sky,
So like a berg of hyaline,
And pencilled blue so daintily,

I never saw her so divine.
But through black branches, rarely drest   20
In scarves of silky shot and shine,

The webbed and the watery west
Where yonder crimson fireball sits
Looks laid for feasting and for rest.

I see long reefs of violets   25
In beryl-covered fens so dim,
A gold-water Pactolus frets

Its brindled wharves and yellow brim,
The waxen colours weep and run,
And slendering to his burning rim   30

Into the flat blue mist the sun
Drops out and all our day is done.

The Habit of Perfection

Elected Silence, sing to me
And beat upon my whorlèd ear,
Pipe me to pastures still and be
The music that I care to hear.

Shape nothing, lips; be lovely-dumb: 5
It is the shut, the curfew sent
From there where all surrenders come
Which only makes you eloquent.

Be shellèd, eyes, with double dark
And find the uncreated light: 10
This ruck and reel which you remark
Coils, keeps, and teases simple sight.

Palate, the hutch of tasty lust,
Desire not to be rinsed with wine:
The can must be so sweet, the crust   15
So fresh that come in fasts divine!

Nostrils, your careless breath that spend
Upon the stir and keep of pride,
What relish shall the censers send
Along the sanctuary side!   20

O feel-of-primrose hands, O feet
That want the yield of plushy sward,
But you shall walk the golden street
And you unhouse and house the Lord.

And, Poverty, be thou the bride   25
And now the marriage feast begun,
And lily-coloured clothes provide
Your spouse not laboured-at nor spun.

God's Grandeur

The world is charged with the grandeur of God.
   It will flame out, like shining from shook foil;
   It gathers to a greatness, like the ooze of oil
Crushed. Why do men then now not reck his rod?
Generations have trod, have trod, have trod;   5
   And all is seared with trade; bleared, smeared with toil;
   And wears man's smudge and shares man's smell: the soil
Is bare now, nor can foot feel, being shod.

And for all this, nature is never spent;
   There lives the dearest freshness deep down things;   10
And though the last lights off the black West went
   Oh, morning, at the brown brink eastward, springs—
Because the Holy Ghost over the bent
   World broods with warm breast and with ah! bright wings.

The Starlight Night

Look at the stars! look, look up at the skies!
   O look at all the fire-folk sitting in the air!
   The bright boroughs, the circle-citadels there!
Down in dim woods the diamond delves! the elves'-eyes!
The grey lawns cold where gold, where quickgold lies!   5
   Wind-beat whitebeam! airy abeles set on a flare!
   Flake-doves sent floating forth at a farmyard scare!—
Ah well! it is all a purchase, all is a prize.

Buy then! bid then!—What?—Prayer, patience, alms, vows.
Look, look: a May-mess, like on orchard boughs!   10
   Look! March-bloom, like on mealed-with-yellow sallows!

These are indeed the barn; withindoors house
The shocks. This piece-bright paling shuts the spouse
   Christ home, Christ and his mother and all his hallows.

The Windhover:

To Christ our Lord

I caught this morning morning's minion, king-
   dom of daylights' dauphin, dapple-dawn-drawn Falcon, in
     his riding
   Of the rolling level underneath him steady air, and striding
High there, how he rung upon the rein of a wimpling wing
In his ecstasy! then off, off forth on swing,   5
   As a skate's heel sweeps smooth on a bow-bend: the hurl
     and gliding
   Rebuffed the big wind. My heart in hiding
Stirred for a bird,—the achieve of, the mastery of the thing!

Brute beauty and valour and act, oh, air, pride, plume, here
   Buckle! AND the fire that breaks from thee then, a billion   10
Times told lovelier, more dangerous, O my chevalier!

   No wonder of it: shéer plód makes plough down sillion
Shine, and blue-bleak embers, ah my dear,
   Fall, gall themselves, and gash gold-vermilion.

The Lantern out of Doors

Sometimes a lantern moves along the night,
   That interests our eyes. And who goes there?
   I think; where from and bound, I wonder, where,
With, all down darkness wide, his wading light?

Men go by me whom either beauty bright   5
   In mould or mind or what not else makes rare:
   They rain against our much-thick and marsh air
Rich beams, till death or distance buys them quite.

Death or distance soon consumes them: wind
   What most I may eye after, be in at the end   10
I cannot, and out of sight is out of mind.

Christ minds; Christ's interest, what to avow or amend
  There, éyes them, heart wánts, care haúnts, foot fóllows
    kind,
Their ránsom, théir rescue, ánd first, fást, last friénd.

The Candle Indoors

Some candle clear burns somewhere I come by.
I muse at how its being puts blissful back
With yellowy moisture mild night's blear-all black,
Or to-fro tender trambeams truckle at the eye.
By that window what task what fingers ply,   5
I plod wondering, a-wanting, just for lack
Of answer the eagerer a-wanting Jessy or Jack
There / God to aggrándise, God to glorify.—

Come you indoors, come home; your fading fire
Mend first and vital candle in close heart's vault: 10
You there are master, do your own desire;
What hinders? Are you beam-blind, yet to a fault
In a neighbour deft-handed? are you that liar
And, cast by conscience out, spendsavour salt?

Felix Randal

Felix Randal the farrier, O he is dead then? my duty all ended,
Who have watched his mould of man, big-boned and hardy-
    handsome
Pining, pining, till time when reason rambled in it and some
Fatal four disorders, fleshed there, all contended?

Sickness broke him. Impatient he cursed at first, but mended 5
Being anointed and all; though a heavenlier heart began some
Months earlier, since I had our sweet reprieve and ransom
Tendered to him. Ah well, God rest him all road ever he
    offended!

This seeing the sick endears them to us, us too it endears.
My tongue had taught thee comfort, touch had quenched thy
    tears,   10
Thy tears that touched my heart, child, Felix, poor Felix Randal;

How far from then forethought of, all thy more boisterous
     years,
When thou at the random grim forge, powerful amidst peers,
Didst fettle for the great grey drayhorse his bright and
     battering sandal!

As kingfishers catch fire, dragonflies dráw fláme;
As tumbled over rim in roundy wells
Stones ring; like each tucked string tells, each hung bell's
Bow swung finds tongue to fling out broad its name;
Each mortal thing does one thing and the same: 5
Deals out that being indoors each one dwells;
Selves—goes itself; *myself* it speaks and spells;
Crying *Whát I dó is me : for that I came.*

Í say móre: the just man justices;
Kéeps gráce: thát keeps all his goings graces;   10
Acts in God's eye what in God's eye he is—
Chríst—for Christ plays in ten thousand places,
Lovely in limbs, and lovely in eyes not his
To the Father through the features of men's faces.

Spelt from Sibyl's Leaves

Earnest, earthless, equal, attuneable, / vaulty, voluminous, . . .
     stupendous
Evening strains to be tíme's vást, / womb-of-all, home-of-all,
     hearse-of-all night.
Her fond yellow hornlight wound to the west, / her wild
     hollow hoarlight hung to the height
Waste; her earliest stars, earl-stars, / stárs principal, overbend
     us,
Fíre-féaturing heaven. For earth / her being has unbound, her
     dapple is at an end, as-   5
tray or aswarm, all throughther, in throngs; / self ín self
     steepèd and páshed—qúite
Disremembering, dísmémbering / áll now. Heart, you round
     me right

(*CARRION COMFORT*)

With: Óur évening is over us; óur night / whélms, whélms, ánd will end us.

Only the beak-leaved boughs dragonish / damask the tool-smooth bleak light; black,

Ever so black on it. Óur tale, O óur oracle! / Lét life, wáned, ah lét life wind   10

Off hér once skéined stained véined varíety / upon, áll on twó spools; párt, pen, páck

Now her áll in twó flocks, twó folds—black, white; / right, wrong; reckon but, reck but, mind

But thése two; wáre of a wórld where bút these / twó tell, each off the óther; of a rack

Where, selfwrung, selfstrung, sheathe-and shelterless, / thóughts agaínst thoughts ín groans grínd.

(Carrion Comfort)

Not, I'll not, carrion comfort, Despair, not feast on thee;
Not untwist—slack they may be—these last strands of man
In me ór, most weary, cry *I can no more*. I can;
Can something, hope, wish day come, not choose not to be.
But ah, but O thou terrible, why wouldst thou rude on me 5
Thy wring-world right foot rock? lay a lionlimb against me? scan
With darksome devouring eyes my bruisèd bones? and fan,
O in turns of tempest, me heaped there; me frantic to avoid thee and flee?

  Why? That my chaff might fly; my grain lie, sheer and clear.
Nay in all that toil, that coil, since (seems) I kissed the rod, 10
Hand rather, my heart lo! lapped strength, stole joy, would laugh, chéer.
Cheer whom though? the hero whose heaven-handling flung me, fóot tród
Me? or me that fought him? O which one? is it each one? That night, that year
Of now done darkness I wretch lay wrestling with (my God!) my God.

No worst, there is none. Pitched past pitch of grief,
More pangs will, schooled at forepangs, wilder wring.
Comforter, where, where is your comforting?
Mary, mother of us, where is your relief?

My cries heave, herds-long; huddle in a main, a chief   5
Woe, world-sorrow; on an age-old anvil wince and sing—
Then lull, then leave off. Fury had shrieked 'No ling-
ering! Let me be fell: force I must be brief'.

  O the mind, mind has mountains; cliffs of fall
Frightful, sheer, no-man-fathomed. Hold them cheap   10
May who ne'er hung there. Nor does long our small
Durance deal with that steep or deep. Here! creep,
Wretch, under a comfort serves in a whirlwind: all
Life death does end and each day dies with sleep.

I wake and feel the fell of dark, not day.
What hours, O what black hoürs we have spent
This night! what sights you, heart, saw; ways you went!
And more must, in yet longer light's delay.
  With witness I speak this. But where I say   5
Hours I mean years, mean life. And my lament
Is cries countless, cries like dead letters sent
To dearest him that lives alas! away.

  I am gall, I am heartburn. God's most deep decree
Bitter would have me taste: my taste was me;   10
Bones built in me, flesh filled, blood brimmed the curse.
  Selfyeast of spirit a dull dough sours. I see
The lost are like this, and their scourge to be
As I am mine, their sweating selves; but worse.

Justus quidem tu es, Domine, si disputem tecum : verumtamen justa loquar ad te :
Quare via impiorum prosperatur? &c.

Thou art indeed just, Lord, if I contend
With thee; but, sir, so what I plead is just.
Why do sinners' ways prosper? and why must
Disappointment all I endeavour end?
    Wert thou my enemy, O thou my friend,   5
How wouldst thou worse, I wonder, than thou dost
Defeat, thwart me? Oh, the sots and thralls of lust
Do in spare hours more thrive than I that spend,
Sir, life upon thy cause. See, banks and brakes
Now, leavèd how thick! lacèd they are again   10
With fretty chervil, look, and fresh wind shakes
Them; birds build—but not I build; no, but strain,
Time's eunuch, and not breed one work that wakes.
Mine, O thou lord of life, send my roots rain.

THOMAS HARDY

Thomas Hardy was born on 2 June 1840 at Higher Bock-hampton, near Dorchester. His father, a master mason, was deeply devoted to music, and as a keen violinist played a leading part in the village orchestra. Hardy's mother was more ambitious than the father and she passed on to her son an intense love of reading and encouraged him in his studies. Even as a child Hardy was a solitary; and at sixteen he appeared to be so frail that his future career was an anxiety to his parents.

The problem was solved by Hardy's being trained as an architect by John Hicks, a Dorchester architect and friend of Hardy's father. Hicks encouraged Hardy to pursue studies other than of a purely architectural nature. While working in Dorchester, Hardy became friendly with William Barnes, the Dorsetshire poet, who kept a school next to Hicks' office. Hardy never lost his admiration and affection for this man to whom he had taken his intellectual problems in early manhood.

Hardy left Hicks to work in London for the distinguished young architect, Arthur Blomfield. Though Hardy achieved a measure of success in London, city life did not suit him, so that he was pleased to return to Bockhampton in 1867. Hardy was a countryman through and through. The bedrock of his whole being was the rural way of life. Not surprisingly, therefore, on his return to Dorset his health returned and he took up the writing of poetry again and considered how he might combine authorship with an architect's practice.

His meeting with Emma Lavinia Gifford at the Rectory of St Juliot in Cornwall while he was engaged on restoration work there led to their marriage in 1874. She was anxious to exchange the narrowly parochial restrictions of rural existence for life in London. After their marriage they lived in Surbiton where Hardy, by this time a novelist with a growing reputation, worked steadily at his writing.

But again London life affected Hardy's health and spirits and, though his wife preferred London, he decided that they should live in a cottage at Sturminster Newton overlooking the River Stour. This was to be their happiest time together. Nevertheless, by 1878, the 'Sturminster Newton Idyll' as Hardy called it was at an end and he returned to London for another five years. He never felt at ease in London and, as a consequence of his established reputation as a novelist, he built himself a house on the outskirts of Dorchester, Max Gate, where he lived for the rest of his life. His first wife died in 1912.

After a period of great desolation and loss, Hardy married, in 1914, Florence Dugdale, a valued family friend. His second wife brought an atmosphere of serenity and devotion to the life of the ageing writer, who had by now achieved national distinction. (He received the Order of Merit in 1910.) He died in 1928, his ashes being buried in Westminster Abbey, though his heart was buried in the grave of his first wife at Stinsford.

It is possible here only to touch upon the important fact that the later years of Hardy's married life with his first wife were unhappy. Conflicting temperaments and beliefs brought division and strain. The 'return of the native' to Sturminster Newton and finally to Max Gate scarcely pleased his wife, with her social aspirations and literary pretensions. Yet their marital relationship had not always been like this. What it had once been and what it unhappily became are the themes of Hardy's most moving poetry.

FURTHER READING

Brown, Douglas. *Thomas Hardy*. Longmans Green, 1961.
Day Lewis, Cecil. *The lyrical poetry of Thomas Hardy* (Wharton Lecture). Oxford University Press, 1953.
Hynes, S. *The pattern of Hardy's poetry*. Oxford University Press, 1961.
McDowell, Arthur. *Thomas Hardy; a critical study*. Faber and Faber, 1931.
Middleton Murry, John. *Aspects of Literature*. Cape, 1934.

Neutral Tones •

We stood by a pond that winter day,
And the sun was white, as though chidden of God,
And a few leaves lay on the starving sod;
　—They had fallen from an ash, and were gray.

Your eyes on me were as eyes that rove　　　　　5
Over tedious riddles of years ago;
And some words played between us to and fro
　On which lost the more by our love.

The smile on your mouth was the deadest thing
Alive enough to have strength to die;   10
And a grin of bitterness swept thereby
    Like an ominous bird a-wing...

Since then, keen lessons that love deceives,
And wrings with wrong, have shaped to me
Your face, and the God-curst sun, and a tree,   15
    And a pond edged with grayish leaves.

At Castle Boterel

As I drive to the junction of lane and highway,
    And the drizzle bedrenches the waggonette,
I look behind at the fading byway,
    And see on its slope, now glistening wet,
        Distinctly yet   5

Myself and a girlish form benighted
    In dry March weather. We climb the road
Beside a chaise. We had just alighted
    To ease the sturdy pony's load
        When he sighed and slowed.   10

What we did as we climbed, and what we talked of
    Matters not much, nor to what it led,—
Something that life will not be balked of
    Without rude reason till hope is dead,
        And feeling fled.   15

It filled but a minute. But was there ever
    A time of such quality, since or before,
In that hill's story? To one mind never,
    Though it has been climbed, foot-swift, foot-sore,
        By thousands more.   20

Primaeval rocks form the road's steep border,
    And much have they faced there, first and last,
Of the transitory in Earth's long order;
    But what they record in colour and cast
        Is—that we two passed.   25

And to me, though Time's unflinching rigour,
  In mindless rote, has ruled from sight
The substance now, one phantom figure
  Remains on the slope, as when that night
    Saw us alight.   30

I look and see it there, shrinking, shrinking,
  I look back at it amid the rain
For the very last time; for my sand is sinking,
  And I shall traverse old love's domain
    Never again.   35

                                      March 1913

Near Lanivet, 1872

There was a stunted handpost just on the crest,
Only a few feet high:
She was tired, and we stopped in the twilight-time for her
    rest,
At the crossways close thereby.

She leant back, being so weary, against its stem,   5
And laid her arms on its own,
Each open palm stretched out to each end of them,
Her sad face sideways thrown.

Her white-clothed form at this dim-lit cease of day
Made her look as one crucified   10
In my gaze at her from the midst of the dusty way,
And hurriedly 'Don't,' I cried.

I do not think she heard. Loosing thence she said,
As she stepped forth ready to go,
'I am rested now. —Something strange came into my
    head,
I wish I had not leant so!'   15

And wordless we moved onward down from the hill
In the west cloud's murked obscure,
And looking back we could see the handpost still
In the solitude of the moor.   20

'It struck her too,' I thought, for as if afraid
She heavily breathed as we trailed;
Till she said, 'I did not think how 'twould look in the shade,
When I leant there like one nailed.'

I, lightly: 'There's nothing in it. For *you*, anyhow!'   25
.. 'O I know there is not,' said she...
'Yet I wonder...if no one is bodily crucified now,
In spirit one may be!'

And we dragged on and on, while we seemed to see
In the running of Time's far glass   30
Her crucified, as she had wondered if she might be
Some day. —Alas, alas!

After a Journey

Hereto I come to view a voiceless ghost;
    Whither, O whither will its whim now draw me?
Up the cliff, down, till I'm lonely, lost,
    And the unseen waters' ejaculations awe me.
Where you will next be there's no knowing,   5
    Facing round about me everywhere,
        With your nut-coloured hair,
And gray eyes, and rose-flush coming and going.

Yes: I have re-entered your olden haunts at last;
    Through the years, through the dead scenes I have
        tracked you;   10
What have you now found to say of our past—
    Scanned across the dark space wherein I have lacked
        you?
Summer gave us sweets, but autumn wrought division?
    Things were not lastly as firstly well
        With us twain, you tell?   15
But all's closed now, despite Time's derision.

I see what you are doing: you are leading me on
    To the spots we knew when we haunted here together,
The waterfall, above which the mist-bow shone
    At the then fair hour in the then fair weather,   20

And the cave just under, with a voice still so hollow
   That it seems to call out to me from forty years ago,
      When you were all aglow,
And not the thin ghost that I now frailly follow!

Ignorant of what there is flitting here to see,   25
   The waked birds preen and the seals flop lazily;
Soon you will have, Dear, to vanish from me,
   For the stars close their shutters and the dawn whitens hazily.
Trust me, I mind not, though Life lours,
   The bringing me here; nay, bring me here again!   30
      I am just the same as when
Our days were a joy, and our paths through flowers.

Pentargan Bay

The Voice

Woman much missed, how you call to me, call to me,
Saying that now you are not as you were
When you had changed from the one who was all to me,
But as at first, when our day was fair.

Can it be you that I hear? Let me view you, then,   5
Standing as when I drew near to the town
Where you would wait for me: yes, as I knew you then,
Even to the original air-blue gown!

Or is it only the breeze, in its listlessness
Travelling across the wet mead to me here,   10
You being ever dissolved to wan wistlessness,
Heard no more again far or near?

   Thus I; faltering forward,
   Leaves around me falling,
Wind oozing thin through the thorn from norward,   15
   And the woman calling.

The Self-unseeing

Here is the ancient floor,
Footworn and hollowed and thin,
Here was the former door
Where the dead feet walked in.

She sat here in her chair,   5
Smiling into the fire;
He who played stood there,
Bowing it higher and higher.

Childlike, I danced in a dream;
Blessings emblazoned that day;   10
Everything glowed with a gleam;
Yet we were looking away!

To an Unborn Pauper Child

Breathe not, hid heart: cease silently,
And though thy birth-hour beckons thee,
Sleep the long sleep:
The Doomsters heap
Travails and teens around us here,   5
And Time-wraiths turn our songsingings to fear.

Hark, how the peoples surge and sigh,
And laughters fail, and greetings die:
Hopes dwindle; yea,
Faiths waste away,   10
Affections and enthusiasms numb;
Thou canst not mend these things if thou dost come.

Had I the ear of wombèd souls
Ere their terrestrial chart unrolls,
And thou wert free   15
To cease, or be,
Then would I tell thee all I know,
And put it to thee: Wilt thou take Life so?

Vain vow! No hint of mine may hence
To theeward fly: to thy locked sense   20
Explain none can
Life's pending plan:
Thou wilt thy ignorant entry make
Though skies spout fire and blood and nations quake.

Fain would I, dear, find some shut plot   25
Of earth's wide wold for thee, where not
One tear, one qualm,
Should break the calm.

But I am weak as thou and bare;
No man can change the common lot to rare.   30

Must come and bide. And such are we—
Unreasoning, sanguine, visionary—
That I can hope
Health, love, friends, scope
In full for thee; can dream thou'lt find   35
Joys seldom yet attained by humankind.

Midnight on the Great Western

In the third-class seat sat the journeying boy,
    And the roof-lamp's oily flame
Played down on his listless form and face,
Bewrapt past knowing to what he was going,
    Or whence he came.   5

In the band of his hat the journeying boy
    Had a ticket stuck; and a string
Around his neck bore the key of his box,
That twinkled gleams of the lamp's sad beams
    Like a living thing.   10

What past can be yours, O journeying boy
    Towards a world unknown,
Who calmly, as if incurious quite
On all at stake, can undertake
    This plunge alone?   15

Knows your soul a sphere, O journeying boy,
    Our rude realms far above,
Whence with spacious vision you mark and mete
This region of sin that you find you in,
    But are not of?   20

Childhood among the Ferns

I sat one sprinkling day upon the lea,
Where tall-stemmed ferns spread out luxuriantly,
And nothing but those tall ferns sheltered me.

3   FCB

The rain gained strength, and damped each lopping frond,
Ran down their stalks beside me and beyond,   5
And shaped slow-creeping rivulets as I conned,

With pride, my spray-roofed house. And though anon
Some drops pierced its green rafters, I sat on
Making pretence I was not rained upon.

The sun then burst, and brought forth a sweet breath   10
From the limp ferns as they dried underneath:
I said: 'I could live on here thus till death';

And queried in the green rays as I sate:
'Why should I have to grow to man's estate,
And this afar-noised world perambulate?'   15

During Wind and Rain

They sing their dearest songs—
He, she, all of them—yea,
Treble and tenor and bass,
   And one to play;
With the candles mooning each face...   5
    Ah, no; the years O!
How the sick leaves reel down in throngs!

They clear the creeping moss—
Elders and juniors—aye,
Making the pathways neat   10
   And the garden gay;
And they build a shady seat...
    Ah, no; the years, the years;
See, the white storm-birds wing across!

They are blithely breakfasting all—   15
Men and maidens—yea,
Under the summer tree,
   With a glimpse of the bay,
While pet fowl come to the knee...
    Ah, no; the years O!   20
And the rotten rose is ript from the wall.

They change to a high new house,
    He, she, all of them—aye,
Clocks and carpets and chairs
    On the lawn all day,   25
And brightest things that are theirs...
    Ah, no; the years, the years;
Down their carved names the rain-drop ploughs.

Friends Beyond

William Dewy, Tranter Reuben, Farmer Ledlow late at plough,
    Robert's kin, and John's, and Ned's,
And the Squire, and Lady Susan, lie in Mellstock churchyard
    now!

'Gone,' I call them, gone for good, that group of local hearts
    and heads;
    Yet at mothy curfew-tide,   5
And at midnight when the noon-heat breathes it back from
    walls and leads,

They've a way of whispering to me—fellow-wight who yet
    abide—
    In the muted, measured note
Of a ripple under archways, or a lone cave's stillicide:

'We have triumphed: this achievement turns the bane to
    antidote;   10
    Unsuccesses to success,
Many thought-worn eves and morrows to a morrow free of
    thought.

No more need we corn and clothing, feel of old terrestrial stress;
    Chill detraction stirs no sigh;
Fear of death has even bygone us: death gave all that we
    possess.'   15

W.D.—'Ye mid burn the old bass-viol that I set such value by.'
Squire—'You may hold the manse in fee,
    You may wed my spouse, may let my children's memory
    of me die.'

3-2

Lady S.—'You may have my rich brocades, my laces; take
  each household key; 20
  Ransack coffer, desk, bureau;
Quiz the few poor treasures hid there, con the letters kept
  by me.'

Far.—'Ye mid zell my favourite heifer, ye mid let the charlock grow,
  Foul the grinterns, give up thrift.'
Far. Wife—'If ye break my best blue china, children, I shan't
  care or ho.'

All—'We've no wish to hear the tidings, how the people's
  fortunes shift; 25
  What your daily doings are;
Who are wedded, born, divided; if your lives beat slow or
  swift.

Curious not the least are we if our intents you make or mar,
  If you quire to our old tune,
If the City stage still passes, if the weirs still roar afar.' 30

—Thus with very gods' composure, freed those crosses late
  and soon
  Which, in life, the Trine allow
(Why, none witteth), and ignoring all that haps beneath the
  moon,

William Dewy, Tranter Reuben, Farmer Ledlow late at
  plough,
  Robert's kin, and John's, and Ned's, 35
And the Squire, and Lady Susan, murmur mildly to me now.

Drummer Hodge

I

They throw in Drummer Hodge, to rest
  Uncoffined—just as found:
His landmark is a kopje-crest
  That breaks the veldt around;
And foreign constellations west 5
  Each night above his mound.

II

Young Hodge the Drummer never knew—
  Fresh from his Wessex home—
The meaning of the broad Karoo,
  The Bush, the dusty loam,   10
And why uprose to nightly view
  Strange stars amid the gloam.

III

Yet portion of that unknown plain
  Will Hodge for ever be;
His homely Northern breast and brain   15
  Grow to some Southern tree,
And strange-eyed constellations reign
  His stars eternally.

W.B.YEATS

William Butler Yeats, the eldest of four children, was born on 13 June 1865 at Sandymount, Co. Dublin. Though he spent his boyhood in London (his father had become a portrait painter, and Yeats grew up in Pre-Raphaelite society in Bedford Park), his childhood memories of Sligo, home of his mother's kin, the Pollexfens, were indelible. Holidays were passed in Sligo with his grandparents or his uncle, George Pollexfen. Joseph Hone writes that 'Sligo, not London, was looked upon by the children as their home and the human being who first loomed large in the poet's life was grandfather Pollexfen, "the silent and fierce old man".'

In 1880 the Yeats family moved back to Howth near Dublin and, after a period at Erasmus High School, Yeats disappointed his father by refusing to enter Trinity College and chose to become an art student at the Metropolitan School of Art, Dublin, where 'A.E.' (George W. Russell, poet and mystic) was a fellow student. Yeats had already begun to write poetry. His first volume of poems, *The Wanderings of Oisin*, was published in 1889, three years after Yeats had abandoned painting. He moved back to London and immersed himself in hermetic studies, theosophy (with Madame Blavatsky), editorial work and the conversation of a circle of friends including Oscar Wilde, G.B. Shaw, William Morris and W.E. Henley. In this year he also met Maud Gonne and the vicissitudes of his long friendship with her form the subject matter of many of his poems. 'In that day', Yeats recollects, 'she seemed a classical impersonation of the Spring, the Virgilian commendation "she walks like a goddess" made for her alone. Her complexion was luminous, like that of apple-blossom through which the light falls, and I remember her standing by a great heap of such blossoms in the window. In the next few years I saw her always when she passed to and fro between Dublin and Paris, surrounded, no matter how rapid her journey and how brief her stay at either end of it, by cages full of birds, canaries, finches of all kinds, dogs, a parrot, and once a full grown hawk from Donegal.' It was this magnificent woman's influence that aroused not only Yeats' love, but his nationalist feelings for Ireland.

In the 'nineties Yeats played a prominent part in the newly founded Rhymers' Club and the Irish Literary Society in London and Dublin. He still pursued his hermetic studies and in 1900 became head of the London branch of the Hermetic Order of the Golden Dawn.

More far-reaching in its effects on Yeats and the Irish literary movement was his introduction to Lady Gregory in 1896, which led to the foundation of the Irish Literary Theatre three years later. This enterprise of a national theatre for Ireland was particularly instrumental in establishing the Irish cultural renaissance. Yeats, John Synge and Lady Gregory devoted all their energies to it. The principle underlying the common undertaking Yeats summed up towards the end of his life in 'The Municipal Gallery Revisited'.

> John Synge, I and Augusta Gregory, thought
> All that we did, all that we said or sang
> Must come from contact with the soil, from that
> Contact everything Antaeus-like grew strong.
> We three alone in modern times had brought
> Everything down to that sole test again,
> Dream of the noble and the beggarman.

In the next two decades Yeats produced most of his finest verse. A new vigour and freshness of utterance characterize the poems of *The Green Helmet* and the succeeding volume, called *Responsibilities* (1914) sets the seal upon this sinewy, trenchant way of writing that encompasses the maximum richness of imagery and forcefulness. His marriage in 1917 to Miss George Hyde-Lees brought Yeats much happiness. His life became 'serene and full of order'. A daughter, Anne Butler Yeats, was born in 1919, and a son, William Michael, in 1921. Public honours were now conferred upon him. He was invited to become a member of the Irish Senate in 1922 and a year later he was awarded the Nobel prize for Literature. He had become the 'sixty-year-old smiling public man'. His health began to fail in the mid 1920s and he was forced to spend much of his life in Italy. He died on Saturday 28 January 1939 at Cap Martin in the south of France and was buried at Rocquebrune. In 1948 his body was brought back to Ireland for reburial in Drumcliff church-yard. On his tombstone this characteristic epitaph is carved:

> Cast a cold eye
> On life, on death.
> Horseman, pass by!

FURTHER READING: BIOGRAPHICAL WORKS

Hone, Joseph. *W. B. Yeats*. Macmillan, 1962.
Jeffares, A. N. *W. B. Yeats : Man and Poet*. Routledge and Kegan Paul, 1962.
Yeats, W. B. *Autobiographies*. Macmillan, 1955.

CRITICAL WORKS

Ellmann, Richard. *The Identity of Yeats*. Macmillan, 1954.
Ellmann, Richard. *Yeats : The Man and the Masks*. Faber and Faber, 1961.
Henn, T. R. *The Lonely Tower*. Methuen, 1965.
Jeffares, A. N. 'The Poetry of W. B. Yeats', in *Studies in English Literature*, 4. Arnold, 1961.
Leavis, F. R. *New Bearings in English Poetry*. Chatto and Windus, 1950.
Melchiori, G. *The Whole Mystery of Art. Pattern into Poetry in the Work of W. B. Yeats*. Routledge and Kegan Paul, 1960.
Stallworthy, Jon. *Between the Lines: Yeats' Poetry in the Making*. The Clarendon Press, Oxford, 1963.
Stock, A. G. *W. B. Yeats : His Poetry and Thought*. Cambridge University Press, 1961.
Unterecker, John. *A Reader's Guide to W. B. Yeats*. Thames and Hudson, 1961.
Ure, Peter. *Yeats*. 'Writers and Critics' Series, Oliver and Boyd, 1963.

The Fascination of What's Difficult

The fascination of what's difficult
Has dried the sap out of my veins, and rent
Spontaneous joy and natural content
Out of my heart. There's something ails our colt
That must, as if it had not holy blood   5
Nor on Olympus leaped from cloud to cloud,
Shiver under the lash, strain, sweat and jolt
As though it dragged road-metal. My curse on plays
That have to be set up in fifty ways,
On the day's war with every knave and dolt,   10
Theatre business, management of men.
I swear before the dawn comes round again
I'll find the stable and pull out the bolt.

The Wild Swans at Coole

The trees are in their autumn beauty,
The woodland paths are dry,
Under the October twilight the water
Mirrors a still sky;

Upon the brimming water among the stones 5
Are nine-and-fifty swans.

The nineteenth autumn has come upon me
Since I first made my count;
I saw, before I had well finished,
All suddenly mount 10
And scatter wheeling in great broken rings
Upon their clamorous wings.

I have looked upon those brilliant creatures,
And now my heart is sore.
All's changed since I, hearing at twilight, 15
The first time on this shore,
The bell-beat of their wings above my head,
Trod with a lighter tread.

Unwearied still, lover by lover,
They paddle in the cold 20
Companionable streams or climb the air;
Their hearts have not grown old;
Passion or conquest, wander where they will,
Attend upon them still.

But now they drift on the still water, 25
Mysterious, beautiful;
Among what rushes will they build,
By what lake's edge or pool
Delight men's eyes when I awake some day
To find they have flown away? 30

In Memory of Major Robert Gregory

I

Now that we're almost settled in our house
I'll name the friends that cannot sup with us
Beside a fire of turf in th' ancient tower,
And having talked to some late hour
Climb up the narrow winding stair to bed: 5
Discoverers of forgotten truth
Or mere companions of my youth,
All, all are in my thoughts to-night being dead.

II

Always we'd have the new friend meet the old
And we are hurt if either friend seem cold,   10
And there is salt to lengthen out the smart
In the affections of our heart,
And quarrels are blown up upon that head;
But not a friend that I would bring
This night can set us quarrelling,   15
For all that come into my mind are dead.

III

Lionel Johnson comes the first to mind,
That loved his learning better than mankind,
Though courteous to the worst; much falling he
Brooded upon sanctity   20
Till all his Greek and Latin learning seemed
A long blast upon the horn that brought
A little nearer to his thought
A measureless consummation that he dreamed.

IV

And that enquiring man John Synge comes next,   25
That dying chose the living world for text
And never could have rested in the tomb
But that, long travelling, he had come
Towards nightfall upon certain set apart
In a most desolate stony place,   30
Towards nightfall upon a race
Passionate and simple like his heart.

V

And then I think of old George Pollexfen,
In muscular youth well known to Mayo men
For horsemanship at meets or at racecourses,   35
That could have shown how pure-bred horses
And solid men, for all their passion, live
But as the outrageous stars incline
By opposition, square and trine;
Having grown sluggish and contemplative.   40

VI

They were my close companions many a year,
A portion of my mind and life, as it were,
And now their breathless faces seem to look
Out of some old picture-book;
I am accustomed to their lack of breath,   45
But not that my dear friend's dear son,
Our Sidney and our perfect man,
Could share in that discourtesy of death.

VII

For all things the delighted eye now sees
Were loved by him: the old storm-broken trees   50
That cast their shadows upon road and bridge;
The tower set on the stream's edge;
The ford where drinking cattle make a stir
Nightly, and startled by that sound
The water-hen must change her ground;   55
He might have been your heartiest welcomer.

VIII

When with the Galway foxhounds he would ride
From Castle Taylor to the Roxborough side
Or Esserkelly plain, few kept his pace;
At Moneen he had leaped a place   60
So perilous that half the astonished meet
Had shut their eyes; and where was it
He rode a race without a bit?
And yet his mind outran the horses' feet.

IX

We dreamed that a great painter had been born   65
To cold Clare rock and Galway rock and thorn,
To that stern colour and that delicate line
That are our secret discipline
Wherein the gazing heart doubles her might.
Soldier, scholar, horseman, he,   70
And yet, he had the intensity
To have published all to be a world's delight.

X

What other could so well have counselled us
In all lovely intricacies of a house
As he that practised or that understood   75
All work in metal or in wood,
In moulded plaster or in carven stone?
Soldier, scholar, horseman, he,
And all he did done perfectly
As though he had but that one trade alone.   80

XI

Some burn damp faggots, others may consume
The entire combustible world in one small room
As though dried straw, and if we turn about
The bare chimney is gone black out
Because the work had finished in that flare.   85
Soldier, scholar, horseman, he,
As 'twere all life's epitome.
What made us dream that he could comb grey hair?

XII

I had thought, seeing how bitter is that wind
That shakes the shutter, to have brought to mind   90
All those that manhood tried, or childhood loved
Or boyish intellect approved,
With some appropriate commentary on each;
Until imagination brought
A fitter welcome; but a thought   95
Of that late death took all my heart for speech.

✛ An Irish Airman Foresees his Death

I know that I shall meet my fate
Somewhere among the clouds above;
Those that I fight I do not hate,
Those that I guard I do not love;
My country is Kiltartan Cross,   5
My countrymen Kiltartan's poor,
No likely end could bring them loss
Or leave them happier than before.

Nor law, nor duty bade me fight,
Nor public men, nor cheering crowds,   10
A lonely impulse of delight
Drove to this tumult in the clouds;
I balanced all, brought all to mind,
The years to come seemed waste of breath,
A waste of breath the years behind   15
In balance with this life, this death.

Easter 1916

I have met them at close of day
Coming with vivid faces
From counter or desk among grey
Eighteenth-century houses.
I have passed with a nod of the head   5
Or polite meaningless words,
Or have lingered awhile and said
Polite meaningless words,
And thought before I had done
Of a mocking tale or a gibe   10
To please a companion
Around the fire at the club,
Being certain that they and I
But lived where motley is worn:
All changed, changed utterly: 15
A terrible beauty is born.

That woman's days were spent
In ignorant good-will,
Her nights in argument
Until her voice grew shrill.   20
What voice more sweet than hers
When, young and beautiful,
She rode to harriers?
This man had kept a school
And rode our wingèd horse;   25
This other his helper and friend
Was coming into his force;
He might have won fame in the end,
So sensitive his nature seemed,

So daring and sweet his thought.   30
This other man I had dreamed
A drunken, vainglorious lout.
He had done most bitter wrong
To some who are near my heart,
Yet I number him in the song;   35
He, too, has resigned his part
In the casual comedy;
He, too, has been changed in his turn,
Transformed utterly:
A terrible beauty is born.   40

Hearts with one purpose alone
Through summer and winter seem
Enchanted to a stone
To trouble the living stream.
The horse that comes from the road,   45
The rider, the birds that range
From cloud to tumbling cloud,
Minute by minute they change;
A shadow of cloud on the stream
Changes minute by minute;   50
A horse-hoof slides on the brim,
And a horse plashes within it;
The long-legged moor-hens dive,
And hens to moor-cocks call;
Minute by minute they live: 55
The stone's in the midst of all.

Too long a sacrifice
Can make a stone of the heart.
O when may it suffice?
That is Heaven's part, our part   60
To murmur name upon name,
As a mother names her child
When sleep at last has come
On limbs that had run wild.
What is it but nightfall?   65
No, no, not night but death;
Was it needless death after all?
For England may keep faith
For all that is done and said.

We know their dream; enough 70
To know they dreamed and are dead;
And what if excess of love
Bewildered them till they died?
I write it out in a verse—
MacDonagh and MacBride 75
And Connolly and Pearse
Now and in time to be,
Wherever green is worn,
Are changed, changed utterly:
A terrible beauty is born. 80

September 25, 1916

On a Political Prisoner

She that but little patience knew,
From childhood on, had now so much
A grey gull lost its fear and flew
Down to her cell and there alit,
And there endured her fingers' touch 5
And from her fingers ate its bit.

Did she in touching that lone wing
Recall the years before her mind
Became a bitter, an abstract thing,
Her thought some popular enmity; 10
Blind and leader of the blind
Drinking the foul ditch where they lie?

When long ago I saw her ride
Under Ben Bulben to the meet,
The beauty of her country-side 15
With all youth's lonely wildness stirred,
She seemed to have grown clean and sweet
Like any rock-bred, sea-borne bird:

Sea-borne, or balanced on the air
When first it sprang out of the nest 20
Upon some lofty rock to stare
Upon the cloudy canopy,
While under its storm-beaten breast
Cried out the hollows of the sea.

The Second Coming

Turning and turning in the widening gyre
The falcon cannot hear the falconer;
Things fall apart; the centre cannot hold;
Mere anarchy is loosed upon the world,
The blood-dimmed tide is loosed, and everywhere   5
The ceremony of innocence is drowned;
The best lack all conviction, while the worst
Are full of passionate intensity.

Surely some revelation is at hand;
Surely the Second Coming is at hand.   10
The Second Coming! Hardly are those words out
When a vast image out of *Spiritus Mundi*
Troubles my sight; somewhere in sands of the desert
A shape with lion body and the head of a man,
A gaze blank and pitiless as the sun,   15
Is moving its slow thighs, while all about it
Reel shadows of the indignant desert birds.
The darkness drops again; but now I know
That twenty centuries of stony sleep
Were vexed to nightmare by a rocking cradle,   20
And what rough beast, its hour come round at last,
Slouches towards Bethlehem to be born?

 ## A Prayer for my Daughter

Once more the storm is howling, and half hid
Under this cradle-hood and coverlid
My child sleeps on. There is no obstacle
But Gregory's wood and one bare hill
Whereby the haystack- and roof-levelling wind,   5
Bred on the Atlantic, can be stayed;
And for an hour I have walked and prayed
Because of the great gloom that is in my mind.

I have walked and prayed for this young child an hour
And heard the sea-wind scream upon the tower,   10
And under the arches of the bridge, and scream
In the elms above the flooded stream;

Imagining in excited reverie
That the future years had come,
Dancing to a frenzied drum,   15
Out of the murderous innocence of the sea.

May she be granted beauty and yet not
Beauty to make a stranger's eye distraught,
Or hers before a looking-glass, for such,
Being made beautiful overmuch,   20
Consider beauty a sufficient end,
Lose natural kindness and maybe
The heart-revealing intimacy
That chooses right, and never find a friend.

Helen being chosen found life flat and dull   25
And later had much trouble from a fool,
While that great Queen, that rose out of the spray,
Being fatherless could have her way
Yet chose a bandy-leggèd smith for man.
It's certain that fine women eat   30
A crazy salad with their meat
Whereby the Horn of Plenty is undone.

In courtesy I'd have her chiefly learned;
Hearts are not had as a gift but hearts are earned
By those that are not entirely beautiful;   35
Yet many, that have played the fool
For beauty's very self, has charm made wise,
And many a poor man that has roved,
Loved and thought himself beloved,
From a glad kindness cannot take his eyes.   40

May she become a flourishing hidden tree
That all her thoughts may like the linnet be,
And have no business but dispensing round
Their magnanimities of sound,
Nor but in merriment begin a chase,   45
Nor but in merriment a quarrel.
O may she live like some green laurel
Rooted in one dear perpetual place.

My mind, because the minds that I have loved,
The sort of beauty that I have approved,   50

4

Prosper but little, has dried up of late,
Yet knows that to be choked with hate
May well be of all evil chances chief.
If there's no hatred in a mind
Assault and battery of the wind   55
Can never tear the linnet from the leaf.

An intellectual hatred is the worst,
So let her think opinions are accursed.
Have I not seen the loveliest woman born
Out of the mouth of Plenty's horn,   60
Because of her opinionated mind
Barter that horn and every good
By quiet natures understood
For an old bellows full of angry wind?

Considering that, all hatred driven hence,   65
The soul recovers radical innocence
And learns at last that it is self-delighting,
Self-appeasing, self-affrighting,
And that its own sweet will is Heaven's will;
She can, though every face should scowl   70
And every windy quarter howl
Or every bellows burst, be happy still.

And may her bridegroom bring her to a house
Where all's accustomed, ceremonious;
For arrogance and hatred are the wares   75
Peddled in the thoroughfares.
How but in custom and in ceremony
Are innocence and beauty born?
Ceremony's a name for the rich horn,
And custom for the spreading laurel tree.   80

June 1919

Sailing to Byzantium

I

That is no country for old men. The young
In one another's arms, birds in the trees,
—Those dying generations—at their song,
The salmon-falls, the mackerel-crowded seas,

Fish, flesh, or fowl, commend all summer long   5
Whatever is begotten, born, and dies.
Caught in that sensual music all neglect
Monuments of unageing intellect.

II

An aged man is but a paltry thing,
A tattered coat upon a stick, unless   10
Soul clap its hands and sing, and louder sing
For every tatter in its mortal dress,
Nor is there singing school but studying
Monuments of its own magnificence;
And therefore I have sailed the seas and come   15
To the holy city of Byzantium.

III

O sages standing in God's holy fire
As in the gold mosaic of a wall,
Come from the holy fire, perne in a gyre,
And be the singing-masters of my soul.   20
Consume my heart away; sick with desire
And fastened to a dying animal
It knows not what it is; and gather me
Into the artifice of eternity.

IV

Once out of nature I shall never take   25
My bodily form from any natural thing,
But such a form as Grecian goldsmiths make
Of hammered gold and gold enamelling
To keep a drowsy Emperor awake;
Or set upon a golden bough to sing   30
To lords and ladies of Byzantium
Of what is past, or passing, or to come.

1927

Leda and the Swan

A sudden blow: the great wings beating still
Above the staggering girl, her thighs caressed
By the dark webs, her nape caught in his bill
He holds her helpless breast upon his breast.

Pzus—✗Leda
Helen g. Troy

How can those terrified vague fingers push   5
The feathered glory from her loosening thighs?
And how can body, laid in that white rush,
But feel the strange heart beating where it lies?

A shudder in the loins engenders there
The broken wall, the burning roof and tower   10
And Agamemnon dead.
                    Being so caught up,
So mastered by the brute blood of the air,
Did she put on his knowledge with his power
Before the indifferent beak could let her drop?

disillusion about what happens to your last in maturity.

✳

Among School Children

I

I walk through the long schoolroom questioning;
A kind old nun in a white hood replies;
The children learn to cipher and to sing,
To study reading-books and histories,
To cut and sew, be neat in everything   5
In the best modern way—the children's eyes
In momentary wonder stare upon
A sixty-year-old smiling public man.

II

I dream of a Ledaean body, bent
Above a sinking fire, a tale that she   10
Told of a harsh reproof, or trivial event
That changed some childish day to tragedy—
Told, and it seemed that our two natures blent
Into a sphere from youthful sympathy,
Or else, to alter Plato's parable,   15
Into the yolk and white of the one shell.

III

And thinking of that fit of grief or rage
I look upon one child or t'other there
And wonder if she stood so at that age—
For even daughters of the swan can share   20

Something of every paddler's heritage—
And had that colour upon cheek or hair,
And thereupon my heart is driven wild:
She stands before me as a living child.

IV

Her present image floats into the mind—   25
Did Quattrocento finger fashion it
Hollow of cheek as though it drank the wind
And took a mess of shadows for its meat?
And I though never of Ledaean kind
Had pretty plumage once—enough of that,   30
Better to smile on all that smile, and show
There is a comfortable kind of old scarecrow.

V

What youthful mother, a shape upon her lap
Honey of generation had betrayed,
And that must sleep, shriek, struggle to escape   35
As recollection or the drug decide,
Would think her son, did she but see that shape
With sixty or more winters on its head,
A compensation for the pang of his birth,
Or the uncertainty of his setting forth?   40

VI

Plato thought nature but a spume that plays
Upon a ghostly paradigm of things;
Solider Aristotle played the taws
Upon the bottom of a king of kings;
World-famous golden-thighed Pythagoras   45
Fingered upon a fiddle-stick or strings
What a star sang and careless Muses heard:
Old clothes upon old sticks to scare a bird.

VII

Both nuns and mothers worship images,
But those the candles light are not as those   50
That animate a mother's reveries,
But keep a marble or a bronze repose.

And yet they too break hearts—O Presences
That passion, piety or affection knows,
And that all heavenly glory symbolise—   55
O self-born mockers of man's enterprise;

VIII

Labour is blossoming or dancing where
The body is not bruised to pleasure soul,
Nor beauty born out of its own despair,
Nor blear-eyed wisdom out of midnight oil.   60
O chestnut-tree, great-rooted blossomer,
Are you the leaf, the blossom or the bole?
O body swayed to music, O brightening glance,
How can we know the dancer from the dance?

In Memory of Eva Gore-Booth and Con Markiewicz

The light of evening, Lissadell,
Great windows open to the south,
Two girls in silk kimonos, both
Beautiful, one a gazelle.
But a raving autumn shears   5
Blossom from the summer's wreath;
The older is condemned to death,
Pardoned, drags out lonely years
Conspiring among the ignorant.
I know not what the younger dreams—   10
Some vague Utopia—and she seems,
When withered old and skeleton-gaunt,
An image of such politics.
Many a time I think to seek
One or the other out and speak   15
Of that old Georgian mansion, mix
Pictures of the mind, recall
That table and the talk of youth,
Two girls in silk kimonos, both
Beautiful, one a gazelle.   20

Dear shadows, now you know it all,
All the folly of a fight

With a common wrong or right.
The innocent and the beautiful
Have no enemy but time;   25
Arise and bid me strike a match
And strike another till time catch;
Should the conflagration climb,
Run till all the sages know.
We the great gazebo built,   30
They convicted us of guilt;
Bid me strike a match and blow.

Coole Park and Ballylee, 1931

Under my window ledge the waters race,
Otters below and moor-hens on the top,
Run for a mile undimmed in Heaven's face
Then darkening through 'dark' Raftery's 'cellar' drop,
Run underground, rise in a rocky place   5
In Coole demesne, and there to finish up
Spread to a lake and drop into a hole.
What's water but the generated soul?

Upon the border of that lake's a wood
Now all dry sticks under a wintry sun,   10
And in a copse of beeches there I stood,
For Nature's pulled her tragic buskin on
And all the rant's a mirror of my mood:
At sudden thunder of the mounting swan
I turned about and looked where branches break   15
The glittering reaches of the flooded lake.

Another emblem there! That stormy white
But seems a concentration of the sky;
And, like the soul, it sails into the sight
And in the morning's gone, no man knows why;   20
And is so lovely that it sets to right
What knowledge or its lack had set awry,
So arrogantly pure, a child might think
It can be murdered with a spot of ink.

Sound of a stick upon the floor, a sound   25
From somebody that toils from chair to chair;

Beloved books that famous hands have bound,
Old marble heads, old pictures everywhere;
Great rooms where travelled men and children found
Content or joy; a last inheritor　　　　　　　　　30
Where none has reigned that lacked a name and fame
Or out of folly into folly came.

A spot whereon the founders lived and died
Seemed once more dear than life; ancestral trees,
Or gardens rich in memory glorified　　　　　　　35
Marriages, alliances and families.
And every bride's ambition satisfied.
Where fashion or mere fantasy decrees
We shift about—all that great glory spent—
Like some poor Arab tribesman and his tent.　　40

We were the last romantics—chose for theme
Traditional sanctity and loveliness;
Whatever's written in what poets name
The book of the people; whatever most can bless
The mind of man or elevate a rhyme;　　　　　45
But all is changed, that high horse riderless,
Though mounted in that saddle Homer rode
Where the swan drifts upon a darkening flood.

Lapis Lazuli

(*For Harry Clifton*)

I have heard that hysterical women say
They are sick of the palette and fiddle-bow,
Of poets that are always gay,
For everybody knows or else should know
That if nothing drastic is done　　　　　　　5
Aeroplane and Zeppelin will come out,
Pitch like King Billy bomb-balls in
Until the town lie beaten flat.

All perform their tragic play,
There struts Hamlet, there is Lear,　　　　　10
That's Ophelia, that Cordelia;
Yet they, should the last scene be there,

The great stage curtain about to drop,
If worthy their prominent part in the play,
Do not break up their lines to weep.   15
They know that Hamlet and Lear are gay;
Gaiety transfiguring all that dread.
All men have aimed at, found and lost;
Black out; Heaven blazing into the head:
Tragedy wrought to its uttermost.   20
Though Hamlet rambles and Lear rages,
And all the drop-scenes drop at once
Upon a hundred thousand stages,
It cannot grow by an inch or an ounce.

On their own feet they came, or on shipboard,   25
Camel-back, horse-back, ass-back, mule-back,
Old civilisations put to the sword.
Then they and their wisdom went to rack:
No handiwork of Callimachus,
Who handled marble as if it were bronze,   30
Made draperies that seemed to rise
When sea-wind swept the corner, stands;
His long lamp-chimney shaped like the stem
Of a slender palm, stood but a day;
All things fall and are built again,   35
And those that build them again are gay.

Two Chinamen, behind them a third,
Are carved in lapis lazuli,
Over them flies a long-legged bird,
A symbol of longevity;   40
The third, doubtless a serving-man,
Carries a musical instrument.

Every discoloration of the stone,
Every accidental crack or dent,
Seems a water-course or an avalanche,   45
Or lofty slope where it still snows
Though doubtless plum or cherry-branch
Sweetens the little half-way house
Those Chinamen climb towards, and I
Delight to imagine them seated there;   50
There, on the mountain and the sky,

On all the tragic scene they stare.
One asks for mournful melodies;
Accomplished fingers begin to play.
Their eyes mid many wrinkles, their eyes,   55
Their ancient, glittering eyes, are gay.

An Acre of Grass

Picture and book remain,
An acre of green grass
For air and exercise,
Now strength of body goes;
Midnight, an old house   5
Where nothing stirs but a mouse.

My temptation is quiet.
Here at life's end
Neither loose imagination,
Nor the mill of the mind   10
Consuming its rag and bone,
Can make the truth known.

Grant me an old man's frenzy,
Myself must I remake
Till I am Timon and Lear   15
Or that William Blake
Who beat upon the wall
Till Truth obeyed his call;

A mind Michael Angelo knew
That can pierce the clouds,   20
Or inspired by frenzy
Shake the dead in their shrouds;
Forgotten else by mankind,
An old man's eagle mind.

Beautiful Lofty Things

Beautiful lofty things: O'Leary's noble head;
My father upon the Abbey stage, before him a raging crowd:
'This Land of Saints', and then as the applause died out,
'Of plaster Saints'; his beautiful mischievous head thrown back.

Standish O'Grady supporting himself between the tables   5
Speaking to a drunken audience high nonsensical words;
Augusta Gregory seated at her great ormolu table,
Her eightieth winter approaching: 'Yesterday he threatened
    my life.
I told him that nightly from six to seven I sat at this table,
The blinds drawn up'; Maud Gonne at Howth station
    waiting a train,   10
Pallas Athene in that straight back and arrogant head:
All the Olympians; a thing never known again.

High Talk

Processions that lack high stilts have nothing that catches the
    eye.
What if my great-granddad had a pair that were twenty foot
    high,
And mine were but fifteen foot, no modern stalks upon
    higher,
Some rogue of the world stole them to patch up a fence or
    a fire.
Because piebald ponies, led bears, caged lions, make but poor
    shows,   5
Because children demand Daddy-long-legs upon his timber
    toes,
Because women in the upper storeys demand a face at the
    pane,
That patching old heels they may shriek, I take to chisel and
    plane.

Malachi Stilt-Jack am I, whatever I learned has run wild,
From collar to collar, from stilt to stilt, from father to
    child.   10
All metaphor, Malachi, stilts and all. A barnacle goose
Far up in the stretches of night; night splits and the dawn
    breaks loose;
I, through the terrible novelty of light, stalk on, stalk on;
Those great sea-horses bare their teeth and laugh at the
    dawn.

The Circus Animals' Desertion

I

I sought a theme and sought for it in vain,
I sought it daily for six weeks or so.
Maybe at last, being but a broken man,
I must be satisfied with my heart, although
Winter and summer till old age began   5
My circus animals were all on show,
Those stilted boys, that burnished chariot,
Lion and woman and the Lord knows what.

II

What can I but enumerate old themes?
First that sea-rider Oisin led by the nose   10
Through three enchanted islands, allegorical dreams,
Vain gaiety, vain battle, vain repose,
Themes of the embittered heart, or so it seems,
That might adorn old songs or courtly shows;
But what cared I that set him on to ride,   15
I, starved for the bosom of his faery bride?

And then a counter-truth filled out its play,
The Countess Cathleen was the name I gave it;
She, pity-crazed, had given her soul away,
But masterful Heaven had intervened to save it.   20
I thought my dear must her own soul destroy,
So did fanaticism and hate enslave it,
And this brought forth a dream and soon enough
This dream itself had all my thought and love.

And when the Fool and Blind Man stole the bread   25
Cuchulain fought the ungovernable sea;
Heart mysteries there, and yet when all is said
It was the dream itself enchanted me;
Character isolated by a deed
To engross the present and dominate memory.   30
Players and painted stage took all my love,
And not those things that they were emblems of.

III

Those masterful images because complete
Grew in pure mind, but out of what began?
A mound of refuse or the sweepings of a street,   35
Old kettles, old bottles, and a broken can,
Old iron, old bones, old rags, that raving slut
Who keeps the till. Now that my ladder's gone,
I must lie down where all the ladders start,
In the foul rag-and-bone shop of the heart.   40

The Man and the Echo

Man

In a cleft that's christened Alt
Under broken stone I halt
At the bottom of a pit
That broad noon has never lit,
And shout a secret to the stone.   5
All that I have said and done,
Now that I am old and ill,
Turns into a question till
I lie awake night after night
And never get the answers right.   10
Did that play of mine send out
Certain men the English shot?
Did words of mine put too great strain
On that woman's reeling brain?
Could my spoken words have checked   15
That whereby a house lay wrecked?
And all seems evil until I
Sleepless would lie down and die.

Echo

Lie down and die.

Man

                    That were to shirk
The spiritual intellect's great work,   20

And shirk it in vain. There is no release
In a bodkin or disease,
Nor can there be work so great
As that which cleans man's dirty slate.
While man can still his body keep   25
Wine or love drug him to sleep,
Waking he thanks the Lord that he
Has body and its stupidity,
But body gone he sleeps no more,
And till his intellect grows sure   30
That all's arranged in one clear view,
Pursues the thoughts that I pursue,
Then stands in judgment on his soul,
And, all work done, dismisses all
Out of intellect and sight   35
And sinks at last into the night.

Echo

Into the night.

Man

O Rocky Voice,
Shall we in that great night rejoice?
What do we know but that we face
One another in this place?   40
But hush, for I have lost the theme,
Its joy or night seem but a dream;
Up there some hawk or owl has struck,
Dropping out of sky or rock,
A stricken rabbit is crying out,   45
And its cry distracts my thought.

EDWARD THOMAS

Edward Thomas was born in Lambeth in 1878. His parents were Welsh; his father, who disapproved of his literary ambitions, was a clerk at the Board of Trade. He went up to Oxford as a non-Collegiate student to read History and was awarded a scholarship by Lincoln College in 1898. In 1899, while still an undergraduate, he married Helen, the daughter of James Ashcroft Noble, the man who had encouraged Thomas in his early nature writing and had helped him to secure publication in magazines and, subsequently, to publish the articles in 1897 in a volume entitled *The Woodland Life*. He married Helen for the excellent reasons that they were in love and she was pregnant.

He began his career as a writer at the age of twenty-two with heavy domestic responsibilities and found himself committed to the disheartening support of Grub Street. Such money as he earned came from reviewing and from books commissioned by many publishers on a great diversity of topics. He wrote critical accounts of Pater and Keats and many volumes on the countryside, in addition to endless reviews. Exacting work of this kind, while it produced a body of fine sensitive prose, left him little time for creative experiment. It was not until 1914, encouraged by his friend Robert Frost, that he began to write poetry. In 1915 he enlisted in the army and found there the leisure and peace of mind which made possible the body of poems he has left. A few were published through the good offices of a friend but he failed to place any himself. Before leaving for France early in 1917, he arranged for 64 of his poems to be published: they appeared a few months after his death at Arras in April 1917. A further 71 were published in 1918, and Faber and Faber published the *Collected Poems* in 1936. There are 141 poems in all.

FURTHER READING: 821.91

Cooke, W. *Edward Thomas*. Faber and Faber, 1970.
Coombes, H. *Edward Thomas*. Chatto and Windus, 1956.
Danby, J. F. 'The Poetry of Edward Thomas'. *The Critical Quarterly*. Winter 1959.

Farjeon, Eleanor. *Edward Thomas : the Last Four Years.* Oxford University Press, 1958.

Moore, John. *The Life and Letters of Edward Thomas.* Heinemann, 1939.

Thomas, Helen. *As It Was* and *World Without End.* Faber and Faber, 1956.

The Owl

Downhill I came, hungry, and yet not starved;
Cold, yet had heat within me that was proof
Against the North wind; tired, yet so that rest
Had seemed the sweetest thing under a roof.

Then at the inn I had food, fire, and rest,   5
Knowing how hungry, cold, and tired was I.
All of the night was quite barred out except
An owl's cry, a most melancholy cry

Shaken out long and clear upon the hill,
No merry note, nor cause of merriment,   10
But one telling me plain what I escaped
And others could not, that night, as in I went.

And salted was my food, and my repose,
Salted and sobered, too, by the bird's voice
Speaking for all who lay under the stars,   15
Soldiers and poor, unable to rejoice.

Swedes

They have taken the gable from the roof of clay
On the long swede pile. They have let in the sun
To the white and gold and purple of curled fronds
Unsunned. It is a sight more tender-gorgeous
At the wood-corner where Winter moans and drips   5
Than when, in the Valley of the Tombs of Kings,
A boy crawls down into a Pharaoh's tomb
And, first of Christian men, beholds the mummy,
God and monkey, chariot and throne and vase,
Blue pottery, alabaster, and gold.   10

But dreamless long-dead Amen-hotep lies.
This is a dream of Winter, sweet as Spring.

October

The green elm with the one great bough of gold
Lets leaves into the grass slip, one by one,—
The short hill grass, the mushrooms small, milk-
    white,
Harebell and scabious and tormentil,
That blackberry and gorse, in dew and sun,   5
Bow down to; and the wind travels too light
To shake the fallen birch leaves from the fern;
The gossamers wander at their own will.
At heavier steps than birds' the squirrels scold.
The rich scene has grown fresh again and new   10
As Spring and to the touch is not more cool
Than it is warm to the gaze; and now I might
As happy be as earth is beautiful,
Were I some other or with earth could turn
In alternation of violet and rose,   15
Harebell and snowdrop, at their season due,
And gorse that has no time not to be gay.
But if this be not happiness,—who knows?
Some day I shall think this a happy day,
And this mood by the name of melancholy   20
Shall no more blackened and obscurèd be.

Ambition

Unless it was that day I never knew
Ambition. After a night of frost, before
The March sun brightened and the South-west blew,
Jackdaws began to shout and float and soar
Already, and one was racing straight and high   5
Alone, shouting like a black warrior
Challenges and menaces to the wide sky.
With loud long laughter then a woodpecker
Ridiculed the sadness of the owl's last cry.
And through the valley where all the folk astir   10
Made only plumes of pearly smoke to tower
Over dark trees and white meadows happier
Than was Elysium in that happy hour,

A train that roared along raised after it
And carried with it a motionless white bower   15
Of purest cloud, from end to end close-knit,
So fair it touched the roar with silence. Time
Was powerless while that lasted. I could sit
And think I had made the loveliness of prime,
Breathed its life into it and were its lord,   20
And no mind lived save this 'twixt clouds and rime.
Omnipotent I was, nor even deplored
That I did nothing. But the end fell like a bell:
The bower was scattered; far off the train roared.
But if this was ambition I cannot tell.   25
What 'twas ambition for I know not well.

Sedge-warblers

This beauty made me dream there was a time
Long past and irrecoverable, a clime
Where any brook so radiant racing clear
Through buttercup and kingcup bright as brass
But gentle, nourishing the meadow grass   5
That leans and scurries in the wind, would bear
Another beauty, divine and feminine,
Child to the sun, a nymph whose soul unstained
Could love all day, and never hate or tire,
A lover of mortal or immortal kin.   10

And yet, rid of this dream, ere I had drained
Its poison, quieted was my desire
So that I only looked into the water,
Clearer than any goddess or man's daughter,
And hearkened while it combed the dark green hair   15
And shook the millions of the blossoms white
Of water-crowfoot, and curdled to one sheet
The flowers fallen from the chestnuts in the park
Far off. And sedge-warblers, clinging so light
To willow twigs, sang longer than the lark,   20
Quick, shrill, or grating, a song to match the heat
Of the strong sun, nor less the water's cool,
Gushing through narrows, swirling in the pool.
Their song that lacks all words, all melody,

All sweetness almost, was dearer then to me   25
Than sweetest voice that sings in tune sweet words.
This was the best of May—the small brown birds
Wisely reiterating endlessly
What no man learnt yet, in or out of school.

Liberty

The last light has gone out of the world, except
This moonlight lying on the grass like frost
Beyond the brink of the tall elm's shadow.
It is as if everything else had slept
Many an age, unforgotten and lost—   5
The men that were, the things done, long ago,
All I have thought; and but the moon and I
Live yet and here stand idle over a grave
Where all is buried. Both have liberty
To dream what we could do if we were free   10
To do some thing we had desired long,
The moon and I. There's none less free than who
Does nothing and has nothing else to do,
Being free only for what is not to his mind,
And nothing is to his mind. If every hour   15
Like this one passing that I have spent among
The wiser others when I have forgot
To wonder whether I was free or not,
Were piled before me, and not lost behind,
And I could take and carry them away   20
I should be rich; or if I had the power
To wipe out every one and not again
Regret, I should be rich to be so poor.
And yet I still am half in love with pain,
With what is imperfect, with both tears and mirth,   25
With things that have an end, with life and earth,
And this moon that leaves me dark within the door.

Old Man

Old Man, or Lad's-love,—in the name there's nothing
To one that knows not Lad's-love, or Old Man,
The hoar-green feathery herb, almost a tree,
Growing with rosemary and lavender.
Even to one that knows it well, the names   5
Half decorate, half perplex, the thing it is:
At least, what that is clings not to the names
In spite of time. And yet I like the names.

The herb itself I like not, but for certain
I love it, as some day the child will love it   10
Who plucks a feather from the door-side bush
Whenever she goes in or out of the house.
Often she waits there, snipping the tips and shrivelling
The shreds at last on to the path, perhaps
Thinking, perhaps of nothing, till she sniffs   15
Her fingers and runs off. The bush is still
But half as tall as she, though it is as old;
So well she clips it. Not a word she says;
And I can only wonder how much hereafter
She will remember, with that bitter scent,   20
Of garden rows, and ancient damson trees
Topping a hedge, a bent path to a door,
A low thick bush beside the door, and me
Forbidding her to pick.
             As for myself,
Where first I met the bitter scent is lost.   25
I, too, often shrivel the grey shreds,
Sniff them and think and sniff again and try
Once more to think what it is I am remembering,
Always in vain. I cannot like the scent,
Yet I would rather give up others more sweet,   30
With no meaning, than this bitter one.

I have mislaid the key. I sniff the spray
And think of nothing; I see and I hear nothing;
Yet seem, too, to be listening, lying in wait
For what I should, yet never can, remember: 35
No garden appears, no path, no hoar-green bush

Of Lad's-love, or Old Man, no child beside,
Neither father nor mother, nor any playmate;
Only an avenue, dark, nameless, without end.

As the Team's Head-brass

As the team's head-brass flashed out on the turn
The lovers disappeared into the wood.
I sat among the boughs of the fallen elm
That strewed the angle of the fallow, and
Watched the plough narrowing a yellow square   5
Of charlock. Every time the horses turned
Instead of treading me down, the ploughman leaned
Upon the handles to say or ask a word,
About the weather, next about the war.
Scraping the share he faced towards the wood,   10
And screwed along the furrow till the brass flashed
Once more.
        The blizzard felled the elm whose crest
I sat in, by a woodpecker's round hole,
The ploughman said. 'When will they take it away?'
'When the war's over.' So the talk began—   15
One minute and an interval of ten,
A minute more and the same interval.
'Have you been out?' 'No.' 'And don't want to,
   perhaps?'
'If I could only come back again, I should.
I could spare an arm. I shouldn't want to lose   20
A leg. If I should lose my head, why, so,
I should want nothing more...Have many gone
From here?' 'Yes.' 'Many lost?' 'Yes, a good few.
Only two teams work on the farm this year.
One of my mates is dead. The second day   25
In France they killed him. It was back in March,
The very night of the blizzard, too. Now if
He had stayed here we should have moved the tree.'
'And I should not have sat here. Everything
Would have been different. For it would have been   30
Another world.' 'Ay, and a better, though
If we could see all all might seem good.' Then
The lovers came out of the wood again:

The horses started and for the last time
I watched the clods crumble and topple over   35
After the ploughshare and the stumbling team.

Lights Out

I have come to the borders of sleep,
The unfathomable deep
Forest where all must lose
Their way, however straight,
Or winding, soon or late;   5
They cannot choose.

Many a road and track
That, since the dawn's first crack,
Up to the forest brink,
Deceived the travellers,   10
Suddenly now blurs,
And in they sink.

Here love ends,
Despair, ambition ends;
All pleasure and all trouble,   15
Although most sweet or bitter,
Here ends in sleep that is sweeter
Than tasks most noble.

There is not any book
Or face of dearest look   20
That I would not turn from now
To go into the unknown
I must enter, and leave, alone,
I know not how.

The tall forest towers;   25
Its cloudy foliage lowers
Ahead, shelf above shelf;
Its silence I hear and obey
That I may lose my way
And myself.   30

Cock-crow

Out of the wood of thoughts that grows by night
To be cut down by the sharp axe of light,—
Out of the night, two cocks together crow,
Cleaving the darkness with a silver blow:
And bright before my eyes twin trumpeters stand,   5
Heralds of splendour, one at either hand,
Each facing each as in a coat of arms:
The milkers lace their boots up at the farms.

WALTER DE LA MARE

Of Huguenot descent, Walter de la Mare was born at Charlton in Kent on 25 April 1873. He was educated at the choir school of St Paul's Cathedral. As a schoolboy he started the school's paper *The Choristers' Journal*. In 1890 he entered the offices of the Anglo-American Oil Company where he worked until 1908. During these years he wrote stories and poems which established his reputation as a poet and writer. A civil list pension in 1908 enabled him to give up his work in business and to devote himself wholly to writing. *Songs of Childhood* was published in 1902, followed by a novel, *Henry Brocken*, in 1904. A further volume of poems was published in 1906. These writings appeared under his pen-name 'Walter Ramal'; but he dropped this after writing became his whole concern. He continued to write a great deal of poetry and many short stories, fantastic, strange and menacing, up to 1955. He also compiled fine anthologies such as *Come Hither*, *Behold this Dreamer* and *Love*.

In 1948 he was made a Companion of Honour and was awarded the Order of Merit in the Coronation honours. He was also awarded a number of honorary degrees from the Universities of Cambridge, St Andrews, Bristol and London. He was elected to membership of the American Academy of Arts and Letters in 1955, a year before his death on 22 June 1956.

As *The Times* rightly said, 'The peculiar quality of Walter de la Mare lay in his combination of the child and the man. He began and he ended, it has been said, in wonder...The world of dream and vision was as real to him as the world of sense.'

FURTHER READING

Atkins, J. A. *Walter de la Mare : an Exploration*. C. and J. Temple, 1947.

Mégroz, R. L. *Walter de la Mare : a Biographical and Critical Study*. Hodder and Stoughton, 1924.

Priestley, J. B., David Cecil, Graham Greene *et al. Tribute to Walter de la Mare on His Seventy-fifth Birthday*. Faber and Faber, 1948.

Reid, Forrest. *Walter de la Mare : a Critical Study*. Faber and Faber, 1929.

The relevant essays in the following works should also be consulted:

Ford, Boris (ed.). *Young Writers, Young Readers*. Hutchinson, 1960.

Leavis, F. R. *New Bearings in English Poetry*. Chatto and Windus, 1950.

Middleton Murry, J. *Countries of the Mind*. Oxford University Press, 1931.

They Told Me

They told me Pan was dead, but I
    Oft marvelled who it was that sang
Down the green valleys languidly
    Where the grey elder-thickets hang.

Sometimes I thought it was a bird   5
    My soul had charged with sorcery;
Sometimes it seemed my own heart heard
    Inland the sorrow of the sea.

But even where the primrose sets
    The seal of her pale loveliness,   10
I found amid the violets
    Tears of an antique bitterness.

All that's Past

Very old are the woods;
    And the buds that break
Out of the brier's boughs,
    When March winds wake,
So old with their beauty are—   5
    Oh, no man knows
Through what wild centuries
    Roves back the rose.

Very old are the brooks;
    And the rills that rise   10
Where snow sleeps cold beneath
    The azure skies
Sing such a history
    Of come and gone,
Their every drop is as wise   15
    As Solomon.

Very old are we men;
    Our dreams are tales
Told in dim Eden
    By Eve's nightingales;   20

We wake and whisper awhile,
    But, the day gone by,
Silence and sleep like fields
    Of amaranth lie.

Fare Well

When I lie where shades of darkness
Shall no more assail mine eyes,
Nor the rain make lamentation
    When the wind sighs,
How will fare the world whose wonder   5
Was the very proof of me?
Memory fades, must the remembered
    Perishing be?

Oh, when this my dust surrenders
Hand, foot, lip, to dust again,   10
May these loved and loving faces
    Please other men!
May the rusting harvest hedgerow
Still the Traveller's Joy entwine,
And as happy children gather   15
    Posies once mine.

Look thy last on all things lovely,
Every hour. Let no night
Seal thy sense in deathly slumber
    Till to delight   20
Thou have paid thy utmost blessing;
Since that all things thou wouldst praise
Beauty took from those who loved them
    In other days.

Gold

Sighed the wind to the wheat:—
'The Queen who is slumbering there,
Once bewildered the rose;
Scorned, "Thou un-fair!"
Once, from that bird-whirring court,   5
Ascended the ruinous stair.

Aloft, on that weed-hung turret, suns
Smote on her hair—
Of a gold by Archiac sought,
Of a gold sea-hid,   10
Of a gold that from core of quartz
No flame shall bid
Pour into light of the air
For God's Jews to see.'

Mocked the wheat to the wind:—   15
'Kiss me! Kiss me!'

I Sit Alone

I sit alone,
And clear thoughts move in me,
Pictures, now near, now far,
Of transient fantasy.
Happy I am, at peace   5
In my own company.

Yet life is a dread thing, too,
Dark with horror and fear.
Beauty's fingers grow cold,
Sad cries I hear,   10
Death with a stony gaze
Is ever near.

Lost in myself I hide
From the cold unknown:
Lost, like a world cast forth   15
Into space star-sown:
And the songs of the morning are stilled,
And delight in them flown.

So even the tender and dear
Like phantoms through memory stray—   20
Creations of sweet desire,
That faith can alone bid stay:
They cast off the cloak of the real
And vanish away.

Only love can redeem   25
This truth, that delight;
Bring morning to blossom again
Out of plague-ridden night;
Restore to the lost the found,
To the blinded, sight.   30

Arabia

Far are the shades of Arabia,
  Where the Princes ride at noon,
'Mid the verdurous vales and thickets,
  Under the ghost of the moon;
And so dark is that vaulted purple   5
  Flowers in the forest rise
And toss into blossom 'gainst the phantom stars
  Pale in the noonday skies.

Sweet is the music of Arabia
  In my heart, when out of dreams   10
I still in the thin clear mirk of dawn
  Descry her gliding streams;
Hear her strange lutes on the green banks
  Ring loud with the grief and delight
Of the dim-silked, dark-haired Musicians 15
  In the brooding silence of night.

They haunt me—her lutes and her forests;
  No beauty on earth I see
But shadowed with that dream recalls
  Her loveliness to me;   20
Still eyes look coldly upon me,
  Cold voices whisper and say—
'He is crazed with the spell of far Arabia,
  They have stolen his wits away.'

Music

When music sounds, gone is the earth I know,
And all her lovely things even lovelier grow;
Her flowers in vision flame, her forest trees
Life burdened branches, stilled with ecstasies.

When music sounds, out of the water rise   5
Naiads whose beauty dims my waking eyes,
Rapt in strange dreams burns each enchanted face,
With solemn echoing stirs their dwelling-place.

When music sounds, all that I was I am
Ere to this haunt of brooding dust I came;   10
While from Time's woods break into distant song
The swift-winged hours, as I hasten along.

'Maerchen' (Fairy Tale)

Soundless the moth-flit, crisp the death-watch tick;
Crazed in her shaken arbour bird did sing;
Slow wreathed the grease adown from soot-clogged wick:
   The Cat looked long and softly at the King.

Mouse frisked and scampered, leapt, gnawed, squeaked; 5
Small at the window looped cowled bat a-wing;
The dim-lit rafters with the night-mist reeked:
   The Cat looked long and softly at the King.

O wondrous robe enstarred, in night dyed deep:
O air scarce-stirred with the Court's far junketing: 10
O stagnant Royalty—A-swoon? Asleep?
   The Cat looked long and softly at the King.

The Ghost

'Who knocks?' 'I, who was beautiful,
Beyond all dreams to restore,
I, from the roots of the dark thorn am hither.
   And knock on the door.'

'Who speaks?' 'I—once was my speech   5
   Sweet as the bird's on the air,
When echo lurks by the waters to heed;
   'Tis I speak thee fair.'

'Dark is the hour!' 'Ay, and cold.'
   'Lone is my house.' 'Ah, but mine?'   10
'Sight, touch, lips, eyes yearned in vain.'
   'Long dead these to thine...'

Silence. Still faint on the porch
   Brake the flames of the stars.
In gloom groped a hope-wearied hand   15
   Over keys, bolts, and bars.

A face peered. All the grey night
   In chaos of vacancy shone;
Nought but vast sorrow was there—
   The sweet cheat gone.   20

The Children of Stare

Winter is fallen early
   On the house of Stare;
Birds in reverberating flocks
   Haunt its ancestral box;
   Bright are the plenteous berries   5
   In clusters in the air.

Still is the fountain's music,
   The dark pool icy still,
Whereupon a small and sanguine sun
   Floats in a mirror on,   10
   Into a West of crimson,
   From a South of daffodil.

'Tis strange to see young children
   In such a wintry house;
Like rabbits' on the frozen snow   15
   Their tell-tale footprints go;
   Their laughter rings like timbrels
   'Neath evening ominous:

Their small and heightened faces
   Like wine-red winter buds;   20
Their frolic bodies gentle as
   Flakes in the air that pass,
   Frail as the twirling petal
   From the briar of the woods.

Above them silence lours,   25
   Still as an arctic sea;
Light fails; night falls; the wintry moon
   Glitters; the crocus soon

Will open grey and distracted
On earth's austerity: 30

Thick mystery, wild peril,
Law like an iron rod:—
Yet sport they on in Spring's attire,
Each with his tiny fire
Blown to a core of ardour   35
By the awful breath of God.

The Song of the Mad Prince

Who said, 'Peacock Pie'?
  The old King to the sparrow:
Who said, 'Crops are ripe'?
  Rust to the harrow:
Who said, 'Where sleeps she now?   5
  Where rests she now her head,
Bathed in eve's loveliness'?—
  That's what I said.

Who said, 'Ay, mum's the word';
  Sexton to willow: 10
Who said, 'Green dusk for dreams,
  Moss for a pillow'?
Who said, 'All Time's delight
  Hath she for narrow bed;
Life's troubled bubble broken'?—   15
  That's what I said.

The Old Summerhouse

This blue-washed, old, thatched summerhouse—
Paint scaling, and fading from its walls—
How often, from its hingeless door
I have watched—dead leaf, like the ghost of a mouse,
Rasping the worn brick floor—   5
The snows of the weir descending below,
And their thunderous waterfall.

Fall—fall: dark, garrulous rumour,
Until I could listen no more.

Could listen no more—for beauty with sorrow   10
Is a burden hard to be borne:
The evening light on the foam, and the swans, there;
That music, remote, forlorn.

Tom's Angel

No one was in the fields
But me and Polly Flint,
When, like a giant across the grass,
The flaming angel went.

It was budding time in May,   5
And green as green could be,
And all in his height he went along
Past Polly Flint and me.

We'd been playing in the woods,
And Polly up, and ran   10
And hid her face, and said,
'Tom! Tom! The Man! The Man!'

And I up-turned; and there,
Like flames across the sky,
With wings all bristling, came   15
The Angel striding by.

And a chaffinch overhead
Kept whistling in the tree
While the Angel, blue as fire, came on
Past Polly Flint and me.   20

And I saw his hair, and all
The ruffling of his hem,
As over the clovers his bare feet
Trod without stirring them.

Polly—she cried; and, oh!   25
We ran, until the lane
Turned by the miller's roaring wheel,
And we were safe again.

John Mouldy

I spied John Mouldy in his cellar,
Deep down twenty steps of stone;
In the dusk he sat a-smiling,
   Smiling there alone.

He read no book, he snuffed no candle; 5
The rats ran in, the rats ran out;
And far and near, the drip of water
   Went whisp'ring about.

The dusk was still, with dew a-falling,
I saw the Dog-star bleak and grim, 10
I saw a slim brown rat of Norway
   Creep over him.

I spied John Mouldy in his cellar,
Deep down twenty steps of stone;
In the dusk he sat a-smiling, 15
   Smiling there alone.

An Epitaph

Here lies a most beautiful lady,
Light of step and heart was she;
I think she was the most beautiful lady
That ever was in the West Country.

But beauty vanishes; beauty passes; 5
However rare—rare it be;
And when I crumble, who will remember
This lady of the West Country?

D.H.LAWRENCE

David Herbert Lawrence was born in 1885 at Eastwood in Nottinghamshire. His father was a coalminer; his mother, sensitive and sardonic, belonged really to the lower bourgeoisie... 'spoke King's English without an accent and never in her life could imitate a sentence of the dialect which Lawrence's father spoke'. Lawrence was educated at Nottingham High School and at University College, Nottingham, where he qualified as a school teacher. Shortly after Lawrence had started teaching, the girl who had been the chief friend of his youth, Jessie Chambers, herself a schoolteacher, sent some of his poems to Ford Madox Hueffer, the editor of the *English Review*. Hueffer printed the poems and Lawrence was launched on his literary career. Further poems and stories followed while Lawrence continued to teach at Davidson Road School in Croydon.

Lawrence abandoned teaching in 1912 and henceforth devoted himself wholly to his writing. After travelling in Italy and Germany he was married in July 1914 to Frieda von Richthofen, the former wife of Professor Ernest Weekley of Nottingham University. It is likely that the Lawrences would have left England, but the outbreak of war in August 1914, the suspicion that centred upon Lawrence owing to his wife's German nationality, together with other difficulties, prevented their departure. What Lawrence endured during the 1914–18 war can be surmised from the largely autobiographical chapter called 'Nightmare' in his novel *Kangaroo*. Nevertheless Lawrence continued to write novels, essays and poetry; and the war years saw the publication of one of his most distinguished novels *The Rainbow* (banned, astonishingly, as obscene). Its 'sequel', *Women in Love*, was not published until 1921, though Lawrence had written it in 1916.

At the end of the war, the Lawrences began their extensive travels, in Europe, Ceylon, Australia and Mexico. They never settled for long anywhere, though the letters, essays and novels are sufficient testimony to Lawrence's remarkable understanding of the 'spirit of place' wherever he found himself. Probably the ranch in Taos, New Mexico, which he acquired from a rich American admirer, Mabel Dodge Luhan, in exchange for the manuscript of *Sons and Lovers*, satisfied him as well as any *pied à terre* that he found. The last five years of his life were spent in Italy, Switzerland and France. In 1929 Lawrence became seriously ill with tuberculosis. He died at Vence on 2 March 1930. His body was later taken to Taos and buried there.

FURTHER READING

Beal, Anthony (ed.). *Selected Literary Criticism.* Heinemann, 1955.

Huxley, Aldous (ed.). *The Letters of D. H. Lawrence.* 2 vols., Heinemann, 1932. This edition contains an excellent introduction to Lawrence as a man and as an artist, by Huxley.

Macdonald, E. D. (ed.). *Phoenix : Posthumous Papers of D. H. Lawrence.* Heinemann, 1961.

Sola Pinto, Vivian de, and Roberts, F. Warren (eds.). *The Complete Poems of D.H. Lawrence.* 2 vols., Heinemann, 1964. This edition also contains a balanced critical assessment of Lawrence's poetry.

BIOGRAPHICAL AND CRITICAL WORKS

Alvarez, A. *The Shaping Spirit.* Chatto and Windus, 1958.

Blackmur, R. P. *Language as Gesture : Essays in Poetry.* Allen and Unwin, 1954.

Moore, Harry T. *The Intelligent Heart.* Heinemann, 1955.

E. T.'s *Memoir* has recently been republished. It gives a valuable picture of Lawrence's youth and early manhood.

Discord in Childhood

Outside the house an ash-tree hung its terrible whips,
And at night when the wind rose, the lash of the tree
Shrieked and slashed the wind, as a ship's
Weird rigging in a storm shrieks hideously.

Within the house two voices arose, a slender lash   5
Whistling she-delirious rage, and the dreadful sound
Of a male thong booming and bruising, until it had drowned
The other voice in a silence of blood, 'neath the noise of
    the ash.

Last Lesson in the Afternoon

When will the bell ring, and end this weariness?
How long have they tugged the leash, and strained apart,
My pack of unruly hounds! I cannot start
Them again on a quarry of knowledge they hate to hunt,
I can haul them and urge them no more.   5

No longer now can I endure the brunt
Of the books that lie out on the desks; a full threescore
Of several insults of blotted pages, and scrawl
Of slovenly work they have offered me.
I am sick, and what on earth is the good of it all!   10
What good to them or me, I cannot see!

                    So, shall I take
My last dear fuel of life to heap on my soul
And kindle my will to a flame that shall consume
Their dross of indifference; and take the toll   15
Of their insults in punishment?—I will not!—

I will not waste my soul and my strength for this.
What do I care for all that they do amiss!
What is the point of this teaching of mine, and of this
Learning of theirs? It all goes down the same abyss.   20

What does it matter to me, if they can write
A description of a dog, or if they can't?
What is the point? To us both, it is all my aunt!
And yet I'm supposed to care, with all my might.

I do not, and will not; they won't and they don't; and that's
    all!   25
I shall keep my strength for myself; they can keep theirs as well.
Why should we beat our heads against the wall
Of each other? I shall sit and wait for the bell.

Sorrow

    Why does the thin grey strand
    Floating up from the forgotten
    Cigarette between my fingers,
    Why does it trouble me?

    Ah, you will understand;   5
    When I carried my mother downstairs,
    A few times only, at the beginning
    Of her soft-foot malady.

    I should find, for a reprimand
    To my gaiety, a few long grey hairs   10
    On the breast of my coat; and one by one
    I watched them float up the dark chimney.

Ballad of Another Ophelia

O the green glimmer of apples in the orchard,
Lamps in a wash of rain!
O the wet walk of my brown hen through the stackyard!
O tears on the windowpane!

Nothing now will ripen the bright green apples   5
Full of disappointment and of rain;
Blackish they will taste, of tears, when the yellow dapples
Of autumn tell the withered tale again.

All round the yard it is cluck! my brown hen
Cluck! and the rain-wet wings;   10
Cluck! my marigold bird, and again
Cluck! for your yellow darlings.

For a grey rat found the gold thirteen
Huddled away in the dark.
Flutter for a moment, oh, the beast is quick and keen,   15
Extinct one yellow-fluffy spark!

Once I had a lover bright like running water,
Once his face was open like the sky,
Open like the sky looking down in all its laughter
On the buttercups, and the buttercups was I.   20

What then is there hidden in the skirts of all the blossom?
What is peeping from your skirts, O mother hen?
'Tis the sun that asks the question, in a lovely haste for
    wisdom;
What a lovely haste for wisdom is in men!

Yea, but it is cruel when undressed is all the blossom   25
And her shift is lying white upon the floor,
That a grey one, like a shadow, like a rat, a thief, a rainstorm
Creeps upon her then and ravishes her store!

O the grey garner that is full of half-grown apples!
O the golden sparkles laid extinct!   30
And O, behind the cloud-leaves, like yellow autumn dapples
Did you see the wicked sun that winked?

Grapes

So many fruits come from roses,
From the rose of all roses,
From the unfolded rose,
Rose of all the world.

Admit that apples and strawberries and peaches and pears
    and blackberries   5
Are all Rosaceae,
Issue of the explicit rose,
The open-countenanced, skyward-smiling rose.

What then of the vine?
Oh, what of the tendrilled vine?   10

Ours is the universe of the unfolded rose,
The explicit
The candid revelation.

But long ago, oh, long ago
Before the rose began to simper supreme,   15
Before the rose of all roses, rose of all the world, was even in
    bud,
Before the glaciers were gathered up in a bunch out of the
    unsettled seas and winds,
Or else before they had been let down again, in Noah's flood,
There was another world, a dusky, flowerless, tendrilled world
And creatures webbed and marshy,   20
And on the margin, men soft-footed and pristine,
Still, and sensitive, and active,
Audile, tactile sensitiveness as of a tendril which orientates
    and reaches out,
Reaching out and grasping by an instinct more delicate than
    the moon's as she feels for the tides.

Of which world, the vine was the invisible rose,   25
Before petals spread, before colour made its disturbance,
    before eyes saw too much.
In a green, muddy, web-foot, utterly songless world
The vine was rose of all roses.

GRAPES 73

There were no poppies or carnations,
Hardly a greenish lily, watery faint.   30
Green, dim, invisible flourishing of vines
Royally gesticulate.

Look now even now, how it keeps its power of invisibility!
Look how black, how blue-black, how globed in Egyptian
    darkness
Dropping among his leaves, hangs the dark grape!   35
See him there, the swart, so palpably invisible:
Whom shall we ask about him?
The negro might know a little.
When the vine was rose, Gods were dark-skinned.
Bacchus is a dream's dream.   40
Once God was all negroid, as now he is fair.
But it's so long ago, the ancient Bushman has forgotten more
    utterly than we, who have never known.

For we are on the brink of re-remembrance.
Which, I suppose, is why America has run dry.   45
Our pale day is sinking into twilight,
And if we sip the wine, we find dreams coming upon us
Out of the imminent night.
Nay, we find ourselves crossing the fern-scented frontiers
Of the world before the floods, where man was dark and evasive
And the tiny vine-flower rose of all roses, perfumed,   50
And all in naked communion communicating as now our
    clothed vision can never communicate.

Vistas, down dark avenues,
As we sip the wine.
The grape is swart, the avenues dusky and tendrilled, subtly
    prehensile,
But we, as we start awake, clutch at our vistas democratic,
    boulevards, tramcars, policemen.   55

Give us our own back,
Let us go to the soda-fountain, to get sober.
Soberness, sobriety.
It is like the agonised perverseness of a child heavy with sleep,
    yet fighting, fighting to keep awake;
Soberness, sobriety, with heavy eyes propped open.   60

Dusky are the avenues of wine,
And we must cross the frontiers, though we will not,
Of the lost, fern-scented world:
Take the fern-seed on our lips,
Close the eyes, and go   65
Down the tendrilled avenues of wine and the otherworld.
                                        San Gervasio

The Mosquito

When did you start your tricks,
Monsieur?

What do you stand on such high legs for?
Why this length of shredded shank,
You exaltation?   5

Is it so that you shall lift your centre of gravity upwards
And weigh no more than air as you alight upon me,
Stand upon me weightless, you phantom?

I heard a woman call you the Winged Victory
In sluggish Venice.   10
You turn your head towards your tail, and smile.

How can you put so much devilry
Into that translucent phantom shred
Of a frail corpus?

Queer, with your thin wings and your streaming legs,   15
How you sail like a heron, or a dull clot of air,
A nothingness.

Yet what an aura surrounds you;
Your evil little aura, prowling and casting numbness on my
     mind.
That is your trick, your bit of filthy magic: 20
Invisibility, and the anaesthetic power
To deaden my attention in your direction.

But I know your game now, streaky sorcerer.
Queer, how you stalk and prowl the air
In circles and evasions, enveloping me,   25
Ghoul on wings
Winged Victory.

Settle, and stand on long thin shanks
Eyeing me sideways, and cunningly conscious that I am aware,
You speck. 30

I hate the way you lurch off sideways into the air
Having read my thoughts against you.

Come then, let us play at unawares,
And see who wins in this sly game of bluff.
Man or mosquito. 35

You don't know that I exist, and I don't know that you exist.
Now then!

It is your trump,
It is your hateful little trump,
You pointed fiend, 40
Which shakes my sudden blood to hatred of you:
It is your small, high, hateful bugle in my ear.

Why do you do it?
Surely it is bad policy.
They say you can't help it. 45

If that is so, then I believe a little in Providence protecting
    the innocent.
But it sounds so amazingly like a slogan,
A yell of triumph as you snatch my scalp.

Blood, red blood
Super-magical 50
Forbidden liquor.

I behold you stand
For a second enspasmed in oblivion,
Obscenely ecstasied
Sucking live blood, 55
My blood.
Such silence, such suspended transport,
Such gorging,
Such obscenity of trespass.

You stagger 60
As well you may.
Only your own accursed hairy frailty,

Your own imponderable weightlessness
Saves you, wafts you away on the very draught my anger
    makes in its snatching

Away with a paean of derision,   65
You winged blood-drop.

Can I not overtake you?
Are you not one too many for me,
Winged Victory?
Am I not mosquito enough to out-mosquito you?   70

Queer what a big stain my sucked blood makes
Beside the infinitesimal faint smear of you!
Queer, what a dim dark smudge you have disappeared into!
                    Siracusa

Humming bird

I can imagine, in some otherworld
Primeval-dumb, far back
In that most awful stillness, that only gasped and hummed,
Humming birds raced down the avenues.

Before anything had a soul   5
While life was a heave of Matter, half inanimate,
This little bit chipped off in brilliance
And went whizzing through the slow, vast succulent stems.

I believe there were no flowers then,
In the world where the humming bird flashed ahead of
    creation.   10
I believe he pierced the slow vegetable veins with his long
    beak.

Probably he was big
As mosses, and little lizards, they say, were once big.
Probably he was a jabbing, terrifying monster.

We look at him through the wrong end of the long telescope
    of Time,   15
Luckily for us.

Kangaroo

In the northern hemisphere
Life seems to leap at the air, or skim under the wind
Like stags on rocky ground, or pawing horses, or springy scut-
tailed rabbits.

Or else rush horizontal to charge at the sky's horizon,
Like bulls or bisons or wild pigs.   5

Or slip like water slippery towards its ends,
As foxes, stoats, and wolves, and prairie dogs.

Only mice, and moles, and rats, and badgers, and beavers,
and perhaps bears
Seem belly-plumbed to the earth's mid-navel.
Or frogs that when they leap come flop, and flop to the centre
of the earth.   10

But the yellow antipodal Kangaroo, when she sits up,
Who can unseat her, like a liquid drop that is heavy, and just
touches earth.

The downward drip
The down-urge.
So much denser than cold-blooded frogs.   15

Delicate mother Kangaroo
Sitting up there, rabbit-wise, but huge, plumb-weighted,
And lifting her beautiful slender face, oh! so much more
gently and finely lined than a rabbit's, or than a hare's,
Lifting her face to nibble at a round white peppermint drop
which she loves, sensitive mother Kangaroo.

Her sensitive, long, pure-bred face.   20
Her full antipodal eyes, so dark,
So big and quiet and remote, having watched so many empty
dawns in silent Australia.

Her little loose hands, and drooping Victorian shoulders.
And then her great weight below the waist, her vast pale belly
With a thin young yellow little paw hanging out, and straggle
of a long thin ear, like ribbon,   25
Like a funny trimming to the middle of her belly, thin little
dangle of an immature paw, and one thin ear.

Her belly, her big haunches
And, in addition, the great muscular python-stretch of her tail.

There, she shan't have any more peppermint drops.
So she wistfully, sensitively sniffs the air, and then turns, goes
      off in slow sad leaps   30
On the long flat skis of her legs,
Steered and propelled by that steel-strong snake of a tail.

Stops again, half turns, inquisitive to look back.
While something stirs quickly in her belly, and a lean little
      face comes out, as from a window,
Peaked and a bit dismayed,   35
Only to disappear again quickly away from the sight of the
      world, to snuggle down in the warmth,
Leaving the trail of a different paw hanging out.

Still she watches with eternal, cocked wistfulness!
How full her eyes are, like the full, fathomless, shining eyes
      of an Australian black-boy
Who has been lost so many centuries on the margins of
      existence!   40

She watches with insatiable wistfulness.
Untold centuries of watching for something to come,
For a new signal from life, in that silent lost land of the South.

Where nothing bites but insects and snakes and the sun, small
      life.
Where no bull roared, no cow ever lowed, no stag cried, no
      leopard screeched, no lion coughed, no dog barked,   45
But all was silent save for parrots occasionally, in the haunted
      blue bush.

Wistfully watching, with wonderful liquid eyes.
And all her weight, all her blood, dripping sack-wise down
      towards the earth's centre,
And the live little-one taking in its paw at the door of her
      belly.

Leap then, and come down on the line that draws to the earth's
      deep, heavy centre.   50

Mountain Lion

Climbing through the January snow, into the Lobo Canyon
Dark grow the spruce-trees, blue is the balsam, water sounds
    still unfrozen, and the track is still evident.

Men!
Two men!
Men! The only animal in the world to fear!   5

They hesitate.
We hesitate.
They have a gun.
We have no gun.

Then we all advance, to meet.   10

Two Mexicans, strangers, emerging out of the dark and snow
    and inwardness of the Lobo valley.
What are they doing here on this vanishing trail?

What is he carrying?
Something yellow.
A deer?   15

Qué tiene, amigo?
León—

He smiles, foolishly, as if he were caught doing wrong.
And we smile, foolishly, as if we didn't know
He is quite gentle and dark-faced.   20

It is a mountain lion,
A long, long slim cat, yellow like a lioness.
Dead.

He trapped her this morning, he says, smiling foolishly.

Lift up her face,   25
Her round, bright face, bright as frost.
Her round, fine-fashioned head, with two dead ears;
And stripes in the brilliant frost of her face, sharp, fine dark
    rays,
Dark, keen, fine rays in the brilliant frost of her face,
Beautiful dead eyes.   30

Hermoso es!

They go out towards the open;
We go on into the gloom of Lobo.
And above the trees I found her lair,
A hole in the blood-orange brilliant rocks that stick up, a
    little cave, 35
And bones, and twigs and a perilous ascent.

So, she will never leap up that way again, with the yellow
    flash of a mountain lion's long shoot!
And her bright, striped frost-face will never watch any more,
    out of the shadow of the cave in the blood-orange rock,
Above the trees of the Lobo dark valley-mouth!

Instead, I look out. 40
And out to the dim of the desert, like a dream, never real;
To the snow of the Sangre de Cristo mountains, the ice of
    the mountains of Picoris,
And near across at the opposite steep of snow, green trees
    motionless standing in snow, like a Christmas toy.

And I think in this empty world there was room for me and a
    mountain lion
And I think in the world beyond, how easily we might spare
    a million or two humans 45
And never miss them.
Yet what a gap in the world, the missing white frost-face of
    that slim yellow mountain lion!

Swan

Far-off
at the core of space
at the quick
of time
beats 5
and goes still
the great swan upon the waters of all endings
the swan within vast chaos, within the electron.

For us
no longer he swims calmly 10
nor clacks across the forces furrowing a great gay trail
of happy energy,

nor is he resting passive upon the atoms,
nor flying north desolative icewards
to the sleep of ice,   15
nor feeding in the marshes,
nor honking horn-like into the twilight.—

But he stoops, now
in the dark
upon us;   20
he is treading our women
and we men are put out
as the vast white bird
furrows our featherless women
with unknown shocks   25
and stamps his black marsh-feet on their white and marshy
      flesh.

Things Men Have Made

Things men have made with wakened hands, and put soft
      life into
are awake through years with transferred touch, and go on
      glowing
for long years.
And for this reason, some old things are lovely
warm still with the life of forgotten men who made them.   5

To Women, as far as I'm Concerned

The feelings I don't have I don't have
The feelings I don't have, I won't say I have.
The feelings you say you have, you don't have.
The feelings you would like us both to have, we neither of us
      have.
The feelings people ought to have, they never have.   5
If people say they've got feelings, you may be pretty sure they
      haven't got them.
So if you want either of us to feel anything at all
you'd better abandon all idea of feelings altogether.

Bavarian Gentians

Not every man has gentians in his house
in Soft September, at slow, sad Michaelmas.

Bavarian gentians, big and dark, only dark
darkening the daytime, torch-like with the smoking blueness
    of Pluto's gloom,
ribbed and torchlike, with their blaze of darkness spread
    blue   5
down flattening into points, flattened under the sweep of
    white day
torch-flower of the blue-smoking darkness, Pluto's dark-blue
    daze,
black lamps from the halls of Dis, burning dark blue,
giving off darkness, blue darkness, as Demeter's pale lamps
    give off light,
lead me then, lead the way.   10

Reach me a gentian, give me a torch!
let me guide myself with the blue, forked torch of this flower
down the darker and darker stairs, where blue is darkened on
    blueness
even where Persephone goes, just now, from the frosted
    September
to the sightless realm where darkness is awake upon the
    dark   15
and Persephone herself is but a voice
or a darkness invisible enfolded in the deeper dark
of the arms Plutonic, and pierced with the passion of dense
    gloom,
among the splendour of torches of darkness, shedding darkness
    on the lost bride and her groom.

Shadows

    And if tonight my soul may find her peace
    in sleep, and sink in good oblivion,
    and in the morning wake like a new-opened flower
    then I have dipped again in God, and new-created.

And if, as weeks go round, in the dark of the moon   5
my spirit darkens and goes out, and soft strange gloom
pervades my movements and my thoughts and words
then I shall know that I am walking still
with God, we are close together now the moon's in shadow.

And if, as autumn deepens and darkens   10
I feel the pain of falling leaves, and stems that break in storms
and trouble and dissolution and distress
and then the softness of deep shadows folding, folding
around my soul and spirit, around my lips
so sweet, like a swoon, or more like the drowse of a low, sad
      song   15
singing darker than the nightingale, on, on to the solstice
and the silence of short days, the silence of the year, the
      shadow,
then I shall know that my life is moving still
with the dark earth, and drenched
with the deep oblivion of earth's lapse and renewal.   20

And if, in the changing phases of man's life
I fall in sickness and in misery
my wrists seem broken and my heart seems dead
and strength is gone, and my life
is only the leavings of a life: 25

and still, among it all, snatches of lovely oblivion, and snatches
      of renewal
odd, wintry flowers upon the withered stem, yet new, strange
      flowers
such as my life has not brought forth before, new blossoms
      of me—

then I must know that still
I am in the hands of the unknown God,   30
he is breaking me down to his own oblivion
to send me forth on a new morning, a new man.

EZRA POUND

Ezra Pound was born in Hailey, Idaho, on 30 October 1885. His father was an assayer in the Philadelphia Mint. In 1901, Ezra Pound entered the state University of Pennsylvania where he was strongly influenced by the Professor of American Constitutional History, Herman Ames. 'His courses', Pound wrote thirty-four years later, 'had a vitality outlasting the mere time of his lectures.' After two years at Pennsylvania, Pound changed to Hamilton College, near Clinton in the state of New York, where the 'refined and sympathetic scholarship' of William P. Shepard led Pound to some knowledge of French, Spanish, Italian and Provençal—the Romance languages of which Pound was to make a close and vital study. Professor Ibbetson instructed him in Anglo-Saxon, a study which was to bear fruit later in his masterly and vigorous translation of 'The Seafarer'. Alongside these studies Pound developed a great interest in the English poets of the 1890s and also the poetry of the Canadian poet, Bliss Carman.

Having gained his Ph.D. at Hamilton in 1905, Pound returned to the University of Pennsylvania to receive his M.A. in 1906 and made his first visit to Europe to further his Provençal studies. At Fribourg he met the distinguished Provençal scholar, Emil Levey. When he returned to America in 1907 he was appointed as a teacher at Wabash College, Crawfordsville, Indiana. His appointment lasted until 1908 when, owing to a petty provincial scandal, he was deprived of his post and left America for Venice and London. London became his home for the next twelve years.

His stay in London was important both for himself and those he came into contact with in the artistic and cultural circles of the time. He played a part in the lives of both Yeats and Eliot, acting as a kind of secretary and mentor to Yeats, whose reputation was established, and working hard for the proper recognition of the then virtually unknown poetry of T. S. Eliot. The range of his acquaintance was extraordinarily wide. T. E. Hulme, James Joyce, H.D., Richard Aldington, D. H. Lawrence, Violet Hunt, Ford Madox Hueffer (Ford), Jacob Epstein, Gaudier-Brzeska—the names read like a roll-call of the avant-garde of the second decade of the century. What is remarkable is Pound's gift for discerning and encouraging real distinction among his contemporaries' work. Gaudier-Brzeska was '*the* sculptor' (his work is now receiving due recognition). Pound saw the importance of Joyce's early work and persuaded Harriet Monroe to publish *Ulysses* in instalments in the *Little Review*, recognizing it as Joyce's 'profoundest work' before it was complete. Of T. S. Eliot, 'Confound it, the fellow can write'. In March 1914 he wrote with characteristic enthusiasm to Amy Lowell: 'I don't see why you shouldn't live half the year in London. After all, it's the only sane place for any one to live if they've any pretence at letters.' Jessie Chambers tells us that at a luncheon party at Ford Madox Hueffer's: 'He was the life of the party. He flung out observations that reminded me of his poetry.' (Pound's poetry had been published by Ford Madox Hueffer in his *English Review*). His marriage to Dorothy Shakespear, the daughter of Yeats' friend Olivia Shakespear, took place in 1914.

But Pound became disillusioned with London, and he left in 1921 for Paris, where he lived until 1925, becoming acquainted with the leading European artists and American expatriates like himself. Here he began that study of Economics whose importance was to loom large when he was writing the *Cantos*, emerging as a condemnation of *Usura*: a medieval hatred of capitalism.

His next move was to Rapallo in Italy where his admiration for the emergent Fascist Movement under Mussolini earned him dislike and distrust.

Although he tried to return to the United States at the outbreak of the 1939–45 war, he was prevented from doing so. He was again denied in 1942 owing to the broadcasts he had made during the war over the Rome Radio. These broadcasts were continued until he was arrested by the American Army in 1945 and indicted for treason on thirteen counts. He had been indicted in his absence for these broadcasts by the Grand Jury of the District Court of Columbia. He remonstrated against his indictment through Switzerland. This indictment was superseded by another, after his arrest in October 1945. He was interrogated by the American Army and then taken to Pisa where he was put in a roofless, barbed-wire cage. Searchlights were trained on him at night and people were forbidden to speak to

him. Such conditions precipitated a severe nervous breakdown
and he was flown to Washington to be tried. On the eve of the
trial he was declared mentally unfit to plead and sent to St
Elizabeth's Mental Hospital in Washington where he remained
until he was released in the late 1950s. He now lives with his
daughter and son-in-law in their castle in the Austrian Tyrol.

FURTHER READING: BIOGRAPHICAL WORKS

Fraser, G. S. *Ezra Pound*. 'Writers and Critics Series'. Oliver and Boyd,
   1960.
Hutchins, Patricia. *Ezra Pound's Kensington: an Exploration, 1885–1913*.
   Faber and Faber, 1965.

CRITICAL WORKS

Davie, Donald. *Ezra Pound : Poet as Sculptor*. Routledge and Kegan Paul,
   1965.
Davie, Donald. 'Ezra Pound's *Hugh Selwyn Mauberley*' in vol. 7 of *The Pelican
   Guide to English Literature*, ed. Boris Ford. Penguin Books, 1961.
Eliot, T. S. (ed.) 'Introduction' to *Selected Poems of Ezra Pound*. Faber and
   Faber, 1948.
Kenner, Hugh. *The Poetry of Ezra Pound*. Faber and Faber, 1951.
Stock, Nigel. *Poet in Exile : Ezra Pound*. Manchester University Press, 1964.
Sullivan, J. P. *Ezra Pound and 'Sextus Propertius'*. Faber and Faber, 1965.

The Return

See, they return; ah, see the tentative
   Movements, and the slow feet,
      The trouble in the pace and the uncertain
      Wavering!

See, they return, one, and by one,   5
With fear, as half-awakened;
As if the snow should hesitate
And murmur in the wind,
      and half turn back;
These were the 'Wing'd-with-Awe',
                  Inviolable.   10

Gods of the wingèd shoe!
With them the silver hounds,
            sniffing the trace of air!

Haie! Haie!
   These were the swift to harry;

These the keen-scented; 15
These were the souls of blood.

Slow on the leash,
                    pallid the leash-men!

The Gipsy

'Est-ce que vous avez vu des autres — des camarades — avec des singes ou
des ours?'   A stray gipsy, A.D. 1912

That was the top of the walk, when he said:
'Have you seen any others, any of our lot,
With apes or bears?'
    —A brown upstanding fellow
Not like the half-castes,   5
        up on the wet road near Clermont.
The wind came, and the rain
And mist clotted about the trees in the valley,
And I'd the long ways behind me,
        gray Arles and Biaucaire,
And he said, 'Have you seen any of our lot?'
I'd seen a lot of his lot...
        ever since Rhodez,   10
Coming down from the fair
        of St John,
With caravans, but never an ape or a bear.

The Seafarer

May I for my own self song's truth reckon,
Journey's jargon, how I in harsh days
Hardship endured oft.
Bitter breast-cares have I abided,
Known on my keel many a care's hold,   5
And dire sea-surge, and there I oft spent
Narrow nightwatch nigh the ship's head
While she tossed close to cliffs. Coldly afflicted,
My feet were by frost benumbed.
Chill its chains are; chafing sighs   10
Hew my heart round and hunger begot
Mere-weary mood. Lest man know not
That he on dry land loveliest liveth,

List how I, care-wretched, on ice-cold sea,
Weathered the winter, wretched outcast   15
Deprived of my kinsmen;
Hung with hard ice-flakes, where hail-scur flew,
There I heard naught save the harsh sea
And ice-cold wave, at whiles the swan cries,
Did for my games the gannet's clamour,   20
Sea-fowls' loudness was for me laughter,
The mews' singing all my mead-drink.
Storms, on the stone-cliffs beaten, fell on the stern
In icy feathers; full oft the eagle screamed
With spray on his pinion.
       Not any protector   25
May make merry man faring needy.
This he little believes, who aye in winsome life
Abides 'mid burghers some heavy business,
Wealthy and wine-flushed, how I weary oft   30
Must bide above brine.
Neareth nightshade, snoweth from north,
Frost froze the land, hail fell on earth then,
Corn of the coldest. Nathless there knocketh now
The heart's thought that I on high streams   35
The salt-wavy tumult traverse alone.
Moaneth alway my mind's lust
That I fare forth, that I afar hence
Seek out a foreign fastness.
For this there's no mood-lofty man over earth's midst   40
Not though he be given his good, but will have in his youth
  greed;
Nor his deed to the daring, nor his king to the faithful
But shall have his sorrow for sea-fare
Whatever his lord will.
He hath not heart for harping, nor in ring-having   45
Nor winsomeness to wife, nor world's delight
Nor any whit else save the wave's slash,
Yet longing comes upon him to fare forth on the water.
Bosque taketh blossom, cometh beauty of berries,
Fields to fairness, land fares brisker,   50
All this admonisheth man eager of mood,
The heart turns to travel so that he then thinks
On flood-ways to be far departing.
Cuckoo calleth with gloomy crying.

He singeth summerward, bodeth sorrow, 55
The bitter heart's blood. Burgher knows not—
He the prosperous man—what some perform
Where wandering them widest draweth.
So that but now my heart burst from my breastlock,
My mood 'mid the mere-flood, 60
Over the whale's acre, would wander wide.
On earth's shelter cometh oft to me,
Eager and ready, the crying lone-flyer,
Whets for the whale-path the heart irresistibly,
O'er tracks of ocean; seeing that anyhow 65
My lord deems to me this dead life
On loan and on land, I believe not
That any earth-weal eternal standeth
Save there be somewhat calamitous
That, ere a man's tide go, turn it to twain. 70
Disease or oldness or sword-hate
Beats out the breath from doom-gripped body.
And for this, every earl whatever, for those speaking after—
Laud of the living, boasteth some last word,
That he will work ere he pass onward, 75
Frame on the fair earth 'gainst foes his malice,
Daring ado...
So that all men shall honour him after
And his laud beyond them remain 'mid the English,
Aye, for ever, a lasting life's-blast, 80
Delight 'mid the doughty.
                Days little durable,
And all arrogance of earthen riches,
There come now no kings nor Caesars
Nor gold-giving lords like those gone. 85
Howe'er in mirth most magnified,
Whoe'er lived in life most lordliest,
Drear all this excellence, delights undurable!
Waneth the watch, but the world holdeth.
Tomb hideth trouble. The blade is layed low. 90
Earthly glory ageth and seareth.
No man at all going the earth's gait,
But age fares against him, his face paleth,
Grey-haired he groaneth, knows gone companions,
Lordly men, are to earth o'ergiven, 95
Nor may he then the flesh-cover, whose life ceaseth,

Nor eat the sweet nor feel the sorry,
Nor stir hand nor think in mid heart,
And though he strew the grave with gold,
His born brothers, their buried bodies   100
Be an unlikely treasure hoard.

The River-merchant's Wife: a Letter

While my hair was still cut straight across my forehead
I played about the front gate, pulling flowers.
You came by on bamboo stilts, playing horse,
You walked about my seat, playing with blue plums.
And we went on living in the village of Chokan: 5
Two small people, without dislike or suspicion.

At fourteen I married My Lord you.
I never laughed, being bashful.
Lowering my head, I looked at the wall.
Called to, a thousand times, I never looked back.   10

At fifteen I stopped scowling,
I desired my dust to be mingled with yours
Forever and forever and forever.
Why should I climb the look out?

At sixteen you departed,   15
You went into far Ku-to-yen, by the river of swirling eddies,
And you have been gone five months.
The monkeys make sorrowful noise overhead.

You dragged your feet when you went out.
By the gate now, the moss is grown, the different mosses,   20
Too deep to clear them away!
The leaves fall early this autumn, in wind.
The paired butterflies are already yellow with August
Over the grass in the West garden;
They hurt me. I grow older.   25
If you are coming down through the narrows of the river
    Kiang,
Please let me know beforehand,
And I will come out to meet you
    As far as Cho-fu-Sa.

                                Rihaku

Lament of the Frontier Guard

By the North Gate, the wind blows full of sand,
Lonely from the beginning of time until now!
Trees fall, the grass goes yellow with autumn.
I climb the towers and towers
  to watch out the barbarous land:
Desolate castle, the sky, the wide desert.   5
There is no wall left to this village.
Bones white with a thousand frosts,
High heaps, covered with trees and grass;
Who brought this to pass?
Who has brought the flaming imperial anger?   10
Who has brought the army with drums and with kettledrums?
Barbarous kings.
A gracious spring, turned to blood-ravenous autumn,
A turmoil of wars-men, spread over the middle kingdom,
Three hundred and sixty thousand,   15
And sorrow, sorrow like rain.
Sorrow to go, and sorrow, sorrow returning.
Desolate, desolate fields,
And no children of warfare upon them,
 No longer the men for offence and defence. 20
Ah, how shall you know the dreary sorrow at the North Gate,
With Rihaku's name forgotten,
And we guardsmen fed to the tigers.

Rihaku

Exile's Letter

To So-Kin of Rakuyo, ancient friend, Chancellor of Gen.
Now I remember that you built me a special tavern
By the south side of the bridge at Ten-Shin.
With yellow gold and white jewels, we paid for songs and
  laughter
And we were drunk for month on month, forgetting the kings
  and princes.   5
Intelligent men came drifting in from the sea and from the
  west border,
And with them, and with you especially

There was nothing at cross purpose,
And they made nothing of sea-crossing or of mountain-
        crossing,
If only they could be of that fellowship,   10
And we all spoke out our hearts and minds, and without regret.
And when I was sent off to South Wei,
        smothered in laurel groves,
And you to the north of Raku-hoku,
Till we had nothing but thoughts and memories in common.
And then, when separation had come to its worst,   15
We met, and travelled into Sen-Go,
Through all the thirty-six folds of the turning and twisting
        waters,
Into a valley of the thousand bright flowers,
That was the first valley;
And into ten thousand valleys full of voices and pine-winds. 20
And with silver harness and reins of gold,
Out came the East of Kan foreman and his company.
And there came also the 'True Man' of Shi-yo to meet me,
Playing on a jewelled mouth-organ.
In the storied houses of San-Ko they gave us more Sennin
        music,   25
Many instruments, like the sound of young phoenix broods.
The foreman of Kan Chu, drunk, danced
        because his long sleeves wouldn't keep still
With that music playing,
And I, wrapped in brocade, went to sleep with my head on
        his lap,
And my spirit so high it was all over the heavens,   30
And before the end of the day we were scattered like stars,
        or rain.
I had to be off to So, far away over the waters,
You back to your river-bridge.

And your father, who was brave as a leopard,
Was governor in Hei Shu, and put down the barbarian rabble. 35
And one May he had you send for me,
        despite the long distance.
And what with broken wheels and so on, I won't say it
        wasn't hard going,
Over roads twisted like sheep's guts.

And I was still going, late in the year,
    in the cutting wind from the North,
And thinking how little you cared for the cost,
    and you caring enough to pay it. 40
And what a reception:
Red jade cups, food well set on a blue jewelled table,
And I was drunk, and had no thought of returning.
And you would walk out with me to the western corner of the
    castle,
To the dynastic temple, with water about it clear as blue
    jade, 45
With boats floating, and the sound of mouth-organs and
    drums,
With ripples like dragon-scales, going grass green on the
    water,
Pleasure lasting, with courtezans, going and coming without
    hindrance,
With the willow flakes falling like snow,
And the vermilioned girls getting drunk about sunset, 50
And the water, a hundred feet deep, reflecting green eyebrows
—Eyebrows painted green are a fine sight in young moon-
    light,
Gracefully painted—
And the girls singing back at each other,
Dancing in transparent brocade,
And the wind lifting the song, and interrupting it,
Tossing it up under the clouds.
        And all this comes to an end.
        And is not again to be met with.
I went up to the court for examination, 60
Tried Layu's luck, offered the Choyo song,
And got no promotion,
    and went back to the East Mountains
    White-headed.
And once again, later, we met at the South bridge-head.
And then the crowd broke up, you went north to San palace, 65
And if you ask how I regret that parting;
It is like the flowers falling at Spring's end
  Confused, whirled in a tangle.
What is the use of talking, and there is no end of talking,
There is no end of things in the heart. 70

I call in the boy,
Have him sit on his knees here
   To seal this,
And send it a thousand miles, thinking.   *Rihaku*

Taking Leave of a Friend

Blue mountains to the north of the walls,
White river winding about them;
Here we must make separation
And go out through a thousand miles of dead grass.

Mind like a floating wide cloud,   5
Sunset like the parting of old acquaintances
Who bow over their clasped hands at a distance.
Our horses neigh to each other
    as we are departing.   *Rihaku*

from 'Homage to Sextus Propertius': IX

1 The twisted rhombs ceased their clamour of accompaniment;
The scorched laurel lay in the fire-dust;
The moon still declined to descend out of heaven,

But the black ominous owl hoot was audible.

And one raft bears our fates
                  on the veiled lake towards Avernus   5
Sails spread on Cerulean waters, I would shed tears for two;
I shall live, if she continue in life,
         If she dies, I shall go with her.
Great Zeus, save the woman,
    or she will sit before your feet in a veil, and tell
    out the long list of her troubles.   10

2 Persephone and Dis, Dis, have mercy upon her,
There are enough women in hell,
                  quite enough beautiful women,
Iope, and Tyro, and Pasiphae, and the formal girls of Achaia,
And out of Troad, and from the Campania,
Death has his tooth in the lot,
                Avernus lusts for the lot of them, 15
Beauty is not eternal, no man has perennial fortune,
Slow foot, or swift foot, death delays but for a season.

3 My light, light of my eyes,
                          you are escaped from great peril,
Go back to Great Dian's dances bearing suitable gifts,
Pay up your vow of night watches
                          to Dian goddess of virgins,   20
And unto me also pay debt;
The ten nights of your company you have promised me.

from 'Hugh Selwyn Mauberley': IV

These fought in any case,
and some believing,
                    pro domo, in any case...

Some quick to arm,
some for adventure,
some from fear of weakness,   5
some from fear of censure,
some for love of slaughter, in imagination,
learning later...
some in fear, learning love of slaughter;

Died some, pro patria,
                    non 'dulce' non 'et decor'...   10
walked eye-deep in hell
believing in old men's lies, then unbelieving
came home, home to a lie,
home to many deceits,
home to old lies and new infamy;   15
usury age-old and age-thick
and liars in public places.

Daring as never before, wastage as never before.
Young blood and high blood,
fair cheeks, and fine bodies;   20

fortitude as never before

frankness as never before,
disillusions as never told in the old days,
hysterias, trench confessions,
laughter out of dead bellies.   25

from 'Hugh Selwyn Mauberley': V

There died a myriad,
And of the best, among them,
For an old bitch gone in the teeth,
For a botched civilization,

Charm, smiling at the good mouth,   5
Quick eyes gone under earth's lid,

For two gross of broken statues,
For a few thousand battered books.

from 'Hugh Selwyn Mauberley': Envoi (1919)

Go, dumb-born book,
Tell her that sang me once that song of Lawes:
Hadst thou but song
As thou hast subjects known,
Then were there cause in thee that should condone   5
Even my faults that heavy upon me lie
And build her glories their longevity.

Tell her that sheds
Such treasure in the air,
Recking naught else but that her graces give   10
Life to the moment,
I would bid them live
As roses might, in magic amber laid,
Red overwrought with orange and all made
One substance and one colour   15
Braving time.

Tell her that goes
With song upon her lips
But sings not out the song, nor knows
The maker of it, some other mouth,   20
May be as fair as hers,
Might, in new ages, gain her worshippers,
When our two dusts with Waller's shall be laid,
Siftings on siftings in oblivion,
Till change hath broken down   25
All things save Beauty alone.

Canto II

Hang it all, Robert Browning,
    there can be but the one 'Sordello'.
But Sordello, and my Sordello?
Lo Sordels si fo di Mantovana.
So-shu churned in the sea.
Seal sports in the spray-whited circles of cliff-wash,   5
Sleek head, daughter of Lir,
    eyes of Picasso
Under black fur-hood, lithe daughter of Ocean;
And the wave runs in the beach-groove:
'Eleanor, $\dot{\epsilon}\lambda\dot{\epsilon}\nu\alpha\upsilon\varsigma$ and $\dot{\epsilon}\lambda\dot{\epsilon}\pi\tau o\lambda\iota\varsigma$!'
   And poor old Homer blind, blind, as a bat,   10
Ear, ear for the sea-surge, murmur of old men's voices:
'Let her go back to the ships,
Back among Grecian faces, lest evil come on our own,
Evil and further evil, and a curse cursed on our children,
Moves, yes she moves like a goddess   15
And has the face of a god
    and the voice of Schoeney's daughters,
And doom goes with her in walking,
Let her go back to the ships,
    back among Grecian voices.'
That by the beach-run, Tyro,
  Twisted arms of the sea-god,   20
Lithe sinews of water, gripping her, cross-hold,
And the blue-gray glass of the wave tents them,
Glare azure of water, cold-welter, close cover.
Quiet sun-tawny sand-stretch,
The gulls broad out their wings,
    nipping between the splay feathers;   25
Snipe come for their bath,
    bend out their wing-joints,
Spread wet wings to the sun-film,
And by Scios,
    to left of the Naxos passage,
Naviform rock overgrown,
    algæ cling to its edge,
There is a wine-red glow in the shallows,
    a tin flash in the sun dazzle.   30

The ship landed in Scios,
    men wanting spring-water,
And by the rock-pool a young boy loggy with vine-must,
   'To Naxos? Yes, we'll take you to Naxos,
Cum' along lad.' 'Not that way!'
'Aye, that way is Naxos.'   35
    And I said: 'It's a straight ship.'
And an ex-convict out of Italy
    knocked me into the fore-stays,
(He was wanted for manslaughter in Tuscany)
    And the whole twenty against me,
Mad for a little slave money.   40
    And they took her out of Scios
And off her course...
    And the boy came to, again, with the racket,
And looked out over the bows,
    and to eastward, and to the Naxos passage.
God sleight then, god-sleight: 45
    Ship stock fast in sea-swirl,
Ivy upon the oars, King Pentheus,
    grapes with no seed but sea-foam,
Ivy in scupper hole.
Aye, I, Accœtes, stood there,
    and the god stood by me,
Water cutting under the keel,   50
Sea-break from stern forrards,
    wake running off from the bow,
And where was gunwale, there now was vine-trunk,
And tenthril where cordage had been,
    grape-leaves on the rowlocks,
Heavy vine on the oarshafts,
And, out of nothing, a breathing,
    hot breath on my ankles,   55
Beasts like shadows in glass,
    a furred tail upon nothingness.
Lynx-purr, and heathery smell of beasts,
    where tar smell had been,
Sniff and pad-foot of beasts,
    eye-glitter out of black air.
The sky overshot, dry, with no tempest,
Sniff and pad-foot of beasts,
    fur brushing my knee-skin,   60

Rustle of airy sheaths,
  dry forms in the æther.
And the ship like a keel in ship-yard,
  slung like an ox in smith's sling,
Ribs stuck fast in the ways,
  grape-cluster over pin-rack,
  void air taking pelt.
Lifeless air become sinewed,
  feline leisure of panthers,
Leopards sniffing the grape shoots by scupper-hole, 65
Crouched panthers by fore-hatch,
And the sea blue-deep about us,
  green-ruddy in shadows,
And Lyaeus: 'From now, Acœtes, my altars,
Fearing no bondage,
 Fearing no cat of the wood, 70
Safe with my lynxes,
  feeding grapes to my leopards,
Olibanum is my incense,
  the vines grow in my homage.'
The back-swell now smooth in the rudder-chains,
Black snout of a porpoise
  where Lycabs had been,
Fish-scales on the oarsmen. 75
 And I worship.
I have seen what I have seen.
 When they brought the boy I said:
'He has a god in him,
  though I do not know which god.'
And they kicked me into the fore-stays. 80
I have seen what I have seen:
 Medon's face like the face of a dory,
Arms shrunk into fins. And you, Pentheus,
Had as well listen to Tiresias, and to Cadmus,
  or your luck will go out of you.
Fish-scales over groin muscles, 85
  lynx-purr amid sea...
And of a later year,
  pale in the wine-red algæ,
If you will lean over the rock,
  the coral face under wave-tinge,

8

Rose-paleness under water-shift,
    Ileuthyeria, fair Dafne of sea-bords,
The swimmer's arms turned to branches,   90
Who will say in what year,
    fleeing what band of tritons,
The smooth brows, seen, and half seen,
    now ivory stillness.
So-shu churned in the sea, So-shu also,
    using the long moon for a churn-stick...
Lithe turning of water,
    sinews of Poseidon,
Black azure and hyaline,   95
    glass wave over Tyro,
Close cover, unstillness,
    bright welter of wave-cords,
Then quiet water,
    quiet in the buff sands,
Sea-fowl stretching wing-joints,
    splashing in rock-hollows and sand-hollows
In the wave-runs by the half-dune;
Glass-glint of wave in the tide-rips against sunlight,
    pallor of Hesperus,   100
Grey peak of the wave,
    wave, colour of grape's pulp,

Olive grey in the near,
    far, smoke grey of the rock-slide,
Salmon-pink wings of the fish-hawk
    cast grey shadows in water,
The tower like a one-eyed great goose
    cranes up out of the olive-grove,

And we have heard the fauns chiding Proteus
    in the smell of hay under the olive-trees.   105
And the frogs singing against the fauns
    in the half-light.
And...

from Canto LXXXI

What thou lovest well remains,
                  the rest is dross

What thou lov'st well shall not be reft from thee
What thou lov'st well is thy true heritage
Whose world, or mine or theirs
                              or is it of none?
First came the seen, then thus the palpable   5
    Elysium, though it were in the halls of hell,
What thou lovest well is thy true heritage
What thou lov'st well shall not be reft from thee

The ant's a centaur in his dragon world.
Pull down thy vanity, it is not man   10
Made courage, or made order, or made grace,
    Pull down thy vanity, I say pull down.
Learn of the green world what can be thy place
In scaled invention or true artistry,
Pull down thy vanity,   15
                    Paquin pull down!
The green casque has outdone your elegance.

'Master thyself, then others shall thee beare'
Pull down thy vanity
Thou art a beaten dog beneath the hail,   20
A swollen magpie in a fitful sun,
Half black half white
Nor knowst'ou wing from tail
Pull down thy vanity
·   How mean thy hates   25
Fostered in falsity,
    Pull down thy vanity,
Rathe to destroy, niggard in charity,
Pull down thy vanity,
    I say pull down.   30

T. S. ELIOT

Born in St Louis, Missouri, T. S. Eliot, 1888–1965, was descended on both sides of his family from early English settlers in New England. Andrew Eliot went from the village of East Coker—see the poem of this name—in 1667; and his maternal ancestor Isaac Sterns was one of the original settlers in the Massachusetts Bay Colony in 1630. New England society, its social and intellectual ambience, was as familiar to Eliot as to Henry James, and like James he did not always treat it with reverence. One of his most deeply ingrained memories of Massachusetts, notably the coast, is captured in 'The Dry Salvages'.

Eliot was educated at Harvard which he left in 1910 to study at the Sorbonne—later he studied in Germany and Oxford. He spent the years of the First World War in England where he worked as a schoolmaster, in banking, and finally as an editor and publisher. His first volume of poetry, published in 1917, was greeted with a good deal of critical abuse, hostility which *Gerontion* in 1920 did little to placate. *The Waste Land*, 1922, established his position as a dominant influence in English poetry which was not seriously challenged throughout the remainder of his life. Between 1922 and 1939 he published much important poetry and criticism, including essays on society. During this period, he edited *The Criterion* which was one of the most influential literary quarterlies. Eliot's deep sense of the numinous and his concern for the values of orthodox religion publicly announced in 1927, the year in which he became a British citizen, deeply influenced his writing, notably his poetry and plays, and achieved its finest expression in *Four Quartets*, the poem he completed during the Second World War which is generally regarded as his greatest single work.

FURTHER READING

Many books offer a critique of Eliot's poetry. In naming some, one is simply acknowledging debts to these interpreters. The following books will be found particularly helpful.

Gardner, Helen. *The Art of T. S. Eliot*, Cresset Press, 1949.

Kenner, Hugh. *T. S. Eliot : the Invisible Poet*. W. H. Allen, 1959.

Matthiessen, F. O. *The Achievement of T. S. Eliot*. Oxford University Press, 1958.

Williamson, George. *A Reader's Guide to T. S. Eliot*. Thames and Hudson, 1955.

The Love Song of J. Alfred Prufrock

> *S'io credesse che mia risposta fosse*
> *A persona che mai tornasse al mondo,*
> *Questa fiamma staria senza più scosse.*
> *Ma perciocchè giammai di questo fondo*
> *Non tornò vivo alcun, s'i'odo il vero,*
> *Senza tema d'infamia ti rispondo.*

Let us go then, you and I,
When the evening is spread out against the sky
Like a patient etherised upon a table;
Let us go, through certain half-deserted streets,
The muttering retreats   5
Of restless nights in one-night cheap hotels
And sawdust restaurants with oyster-shells:
Streets that follow like a tedious argument
Of insidious intent
To lead you to an overwhelming question...   10
Oh, do not ask, 'What is it?'
Let us go and make our visit.

In the room the women come and go
Talking of Michelangelo.

The yellow fog that rubs its back upon the window-panes,   15
The yellow smoke that rubs its muzzle on the window-panes
Licked its tongue into the corners of the evening,
Lingered upon the pools that stand in drains,
Let fall upon its back the soot that falls from chimneys,
Slipped by the terrace, made a sudden leap,   20
And seeing that it was a soft October night,
Curled once about the house, and fell asleep.

And indeed there will be time
For the yellow smoke that slides along the street
Rubbing its back upon the window-panes;   25
There will be time, there will be time
To prepare a face to meet the faces that you meet;
There will be time to murder and create,
And time for all the works and days of hands
That lift and drop a question on your plate;   30

Time for you and time for me,
And time yet for a hundred indecisions,
And for a hundred visions and revisions,
Before the taking of a toast and tea.

In the room the women come and go   35
Talking of Michelangelo.

And indeed there will be time
To wonder, 'Do I dare?' and, 'Do I dare?'
Time to turn back and descend the stair,
With a bald spot in the middle of my hair—   40
(They will say: 'How his hair is growing thin!')
My morning coat, my collar mounting firmly to the chin,
My necktie rich and modest, but asserted by a simple pin—
(They will say: 'But how his arms and legs are thin!')
Do I dare   45
Disturb the universe?
In a minute there is time
For decisions and revisions which a minute will reverse.

For I have known them all already, known them all—
Have known the evenings, mornings, afternoons,   50
I have measured out my life with coffee spoons;
I know the voices dying with a dying fall   *modulation of voic*
Beneath the music from a farther room.   *cultured*
   So how should I presume?

And I have known the eyes already, known them all—   55
The eyes that fix you in a formulated phrase,
And when I am formulated, sprawling on a pin,
When I am pinned and wriggling on the wall,
Then how should I begin
To spit out all the butt-ends of my days and ways?   60
   And how should I presume?

And I have known the arms already, known them all—
Arms that are braceleted and white and bare
(But in the lamplight, downed with light brown hair!)
Is it perfume from a dress   65
That makes me so digress?

Arms that lie along a table, or wrap about a shawl.
   And should I then presume?
   And how should I begin?

     .   .   .   .   .   .

Shall I say, I have gone at dusk through narrow streets   70
And watched the smoke that rises from the pipes
Of lonely men in shirt-sleeves, leaning out of windows?...

I should have been a pair of ragged claws
Scuttling across the floors of silent seas.

     .   .   .   .   .   .

And the afternoon, the evening, sleeps so peacefully!   75
Smoothed by long fingers,
Asleep...tired...or it malingers,
Stretched on the floor, here beside you and me.
Should I, after tea and cakes and ices,
Have the strength to force the moment to its crisis?   80
But though I have wept and fasted, wept and prayed,
Though I have seen my head (grown slightly bald) brought
     in upon a platter,
I am no prophet—and here's no great matter;
I have seen the moment of my greatness flicker,
And I have seen the eternal Footman hold my coat, and
     snicker,   85
And in short, I was afraid.

And would it have been worth it, after all,
After the cups, the marmalade, the tea,
Among the porcelain, among some talk of you and me,   *type of society*
Would it have been worth while,   90
To have bitten off the matter with a smile,
To have squeezed the universe into a ball
To roll it toward some overwhelming question,
To say: 'I am Lazarus, come from the dead,
Come back to tell you all, I shall tell you all'—   95
If one, settling a pillow by her head,
   Should say: 'That is not what I meant at all.
   That is not it, at all.'

And would it have been worth it, after all,
Would it have been worth while,   100
After the sunsets and the dooryards and the sprinkled streets,

After the novels, after the teacups, after the skirts that trail
    along the floor—
And this, and so much more?—
It is impossible to say just what I mean!
But as if a magic lantern threw the nerves in patterns on a
    screen: 105
Would it have been worth while
If one, settling a pillow or throwing off a shawl,
And turning toward the window, should say:
  'That is not it at all,
    That is not what I meant, at all.'   110

No! I am not Prince Hamlet, nor was meant to be; *important enough to change society*
Am an attendant lord, one that will do
To swell a progress, start a scene or two,
Advise the prince; no doubt, an easy tool,
Deferential, glad to be of use,   115
Politic, cautious, and meticulous;
Full of high sentence, but a bit obtuse;
At times, indeed, almost ridiculous—
Almost, at times, the Fool.

I grow old...I grow old...   120
I shall wear the bottoms of my trousers rolled.

Shall I part my hair behind? Do I dare to eat a peach? *ironical*
I shall wear white flannel trousers, and walk upon the beach.
I have heard the mermaids singing, each to each.

I do not think that they will sing to me.   125

I have seen them riding seaward on the waves
Combing the white hair of the waves blown back
When the wind blows the water white and black.

We have lingered in the chambers of the sea
By sea-girls wreathed with seaweed red and brown   130
Till human voices wake us, and we drown.

Portrait of a Lady

Thou hast committed—
Fornication : but that was in another country,
And besides, the wench is dead.

The Jew of Malta

I

Among the smoke and fog of a December afternoon
You have the scene arrange itself—as it will seem to do—
With 'I have saved this afternoon for you';
And four wax candles in the darkened room,
Four rings of light upon the ceiling overhead,   5
An atmosphere of Juliet's tomb
Prepared for all the things to be said, or left unsaid.
We have been, let us say, to hear the latest Pole
Transmit the Preludes, through his hair and finger-tips.
'So intimate, this Chopin, that I think his soul   10
Should be resurrected only among friends
Some two or three, who will not touch the bloom
That is rubbed and questioned in the concert room.'
—And so the conversation slips
Among velleities and carefully caught regrets   15
Through attenuated tones of violins
Mingled with remote cornets
And begins.
'You do not know how much they mean to me, my friends,
And how, how rare and strange it is, to find   20
In a life composed so much, so much of odds and ends,
(For indeed I do not love it...you knew? you are not blind!
How keen you are!)
To find a friend who has these qualities,
Who has, and gives   25
Those qualities upon which friendship lives.
How much it means that I say this to you—
Without these friendships—life, what cauchemar!'

Among the windings of the violins
And the ariettes   30
Of cracked cornets
Inside my brain a dull tom-tom begins
Absurdly hammering a prelude of its own,

Capricious monotone
That is at least one definite 'false note.'   35
—Let us take the air, in a tobacco trance,
Admire the monuments,
Discuss the late events,
Correct our watches by the public clocks.
Then sit for half an hour and drink our blocks.   40

II

Now that lilacs are in bloom
She has a bowl of lilacs in her room
And twists one in her fingers while she talks.
'Ah, my friend, you do not know, you do not know
What life is, you who hold it in your hands';   45
(Slowly twisting the lilac stalks)
'You let it flow from you, you let it flow,
And youth is cruel, and has no remorse
And smiles at situations which it cannot see.'
I smile, of course,   50
And go on drinking tea.

    'Yet with these April sunsets, that somehow recall
My buried life, and Paris in the Spring,
I feel immeasurably at peace, and find the world
To be wonderful and youthful, after all.'   55

    The voice returns like the insistent out-of-tune
Of a broken violin on an August afternoon:
'I am always sure that you understand
My feelings, always sure that you feel,
Sure that across the gulf you reach your hand.   60

    You are invulnerable, you have no Achilles' heel.
You will go on, and when you have prevailed
You can say: at this point many a one has failed.
But what have I, but what have I, my friend,
To give you, what can you receive from me?   65
Only the friendship and the sympathy
Of one about to reach her journey's end.

    I shall sit here, serving tea to friends...'

    I take my hat: how can I make a cowardly amends
For what she has said to me?   70

You will see me any morning in the park
Reading the comics and the sporting page.
Particularly I remark
An English countess goes upon the stage.
A Greek was murdered at a Polish dance,   75
Another bank defaulter has confessed.
I keep my countenance,
I remain self-possessed
Except when a street-piano, mechanical and tired
Reiterates some worn-out common song   80
With the smell of hyacinths across the garden
Recalling things that other people have desired.
Are these ideas right or wrong?

III

 The October night comes down; returning as before
Except for a slight sensation of being ill at ease   85
I mount the stairs and turn the handle of the door
And feel as if I had mounted on my hands and knees.
'And so you are going abroad; and when do you return?
But that's a useless question.
You hardly know when you are coming back,   90
You will find so much to learn.'
My smile falls heavily among the bric-à-brac.

 'Perhaps you can write to me.'
My self-possession flares up for a second;
This is as I had reckoned.   95
'I have been wondering frequently of late
(But our beginnings never know our ends!)
Why we have not developed into friends.'
I feel like one who smiles, and turning shall remark
Suddenly, his expression in a glass.   100
My self-possession gutters; we are really in the dark.

 'For everybody said so, all our friends,
They all were sure our feelings would relate
So closely! I myself can hardly understand.
We must leave it now to fate.   105
You will write, at any rate.
Perhaps it is not too late.

I shall sit here, serving tea to friends.'

And I must borrow every changing shape
To find expression...dance, dance   110
Like a dancing bear,
Cry like a parrot, chatter like an ape.
Let us take the air, in a tobacco trance—

Well! and what if she should die some afternoon,
Afternoon grey and smoky, evening yellow and rose;   115
Should die and leave me sitting pen in hand
With the smoke coming down above the housetops;
Doubtful, for a while
Not knowing what to feel or if I understand
Or whether wise or foolish, tardy or too soon...   120
Would she not have the advantage, after all?
This music is successful with a 'dying fall'
Now that we talk of dying—
And should I have the right to smile?

Gerontion

Thou hast nor youth nor age
But as it were an after dinner sleep
Dreaming of both.

Here I am, an old man in a dry month,
Being read to by a boy, waiting for rain.
I was neither at the hot gates
Nor fought in the warm rain
Nor knee deep in the salt marsh, heaving a cutlass,   5
Bitten by flies, fought.
My house is a decayed house,
And the jew squats on the window sill, the owner,
Spawned in some estaminet of Antwerp,
Blistered in Brussels, patched and peeled in London. 10
The goat coughs at night in the field overhead;
Rocks, moss, stonecrop, iron, merds.
The woman keeps the kitchen, makes tea,
Sneezes at evening, poking the peevish gutter.
                                    I an old man,   15
A dull head among windy spaces.

Signs are taken for wonders. 'We would see a sign!'
The word within a word, unable to speak a word,
Swaddled with darkness. In the juvescence of the year
Came Christ the tiger   20

In depraved May, dogwood and chestnut, flowering judas,
To be eaten, to be divided, to be drunk
Among whispers; by Mr. Silvero
With caressing hands, at Limoges
Who walked all night in the next room;   25

By Hakagawa, bowing among the Titians;
By Madame de Tornquist, in the dark room
Shifting the candles; Fraülein von Kulp
Who turned in the hall, one hand on the door. Vacant
    shuttles
Weave the wind. I have no ghosts,   30
An old man in a draughty house
Under a windy knob.

After such knowledge, what forgiveness? Think now
History has many cunning passages, contrived corridors
And issues, deceives with whispering ambitions,   35
Guides us by vanities. Think now
She gives when our attention is distracted
And what she gives, gives with such supple confusions
That the giving famishes the craving. Gives too late
What's not believed in, or if still believed,   40
In memory only, reconsidered passion. Gives too soon
Into weak hands, what's thought can be dispensed with
Till the refusal propagates a fear. Think
Neither fear nor courage saves us. Unnatural vices
Are fathered by our heroism. Virtues   45
Are forced upon us by our impudent crimes.
These tears are shaken from the wrath-bearing tree.

The tiger springs in the new year. Us he devours. Think at last
We have not reached conclusion, when I
Stiffen in a rented house. Think at last   50
I have not made this show purposelessly
And it is not by any concitation
Of the backward devils.

I would meet you upon this honestly.
I that was near your heart was removed therefrom   55
To lose beauty in terror, terror in inquisition.
I have lost my passion: why should I need to keep it
Since what is kept must be adulterated?
I have lost my sight, smell, hearing, taste and touch:
How should I use them for your closer contact?   60

These with a thousand small deliberations
Protract the profit of their chilled delirium,
Excite the membrane, when the sense has cooled,
With pungent sauces, multiply variety
In a wilderness of mirrors. What will the spider do,   65
Suspend its operations, will the weevil
Delay? De Bailhache, Fresca, Mrs. Cammel, whirled
Beyond the circuit of the shuddering Bear
In fractured atoms. Gull against the wind, in the windy
          straits
Of Belle Isle, or running on the Horn,   70
White feathers in the snow, the Gulf claims,
And an old man driven by the Trades
To a sleepy corner.

                              Tenants of the house,
Thoughts of a dry brain in a dry season.   75

Marina   from Periclese Play (Greek?)

Quis hic locus, quae
regio, quae mundi plaga?

What seas what shores what grey rocks and what islands
What water lapping the bow
And scent of pine and the woodthrush singing through the
          fog
What images return
O my daughter.   5

Those who sharpen the tooth of the dog, meaning
Death
Those who glitter with the glory of the hummingbird,
          meaning
Death

Those who sit in the stye of contentment, meaning   10
Death
Those who suffer the ecstasy of the animals, meaning
Death

Are become unsubstantial, reduced by a wind,
A breath of pine, and the woodsong fog   15
By this grace dissolved in place

What is this face, less clear and clearer
The pulse in the arm, less strong and stronger—
Given or lent? more distant than stars and nearer than the
        eye

Whispers and small laughter between leaves and hurrying
        feet   20
Under sleep, where all the waters meet.

Bowsprit cracked with ice and paint cracked with heat.
I made this, I have forgotten
And remember.
The rigging weak and the canvas rotten   25
Between one June and another September.
Made this unknowing, half conscious, unknown, my own.
The garboard strake leaks, the seams need caulking.
This form, this face, this life
Living to live in a world of time beyond me; let me   30
Resign my life for this life, my speech for that unspoken,
The awakened, lips parted, the hope, the new ships.

What seas what shores what granite islands towards my
        timbers
And woodthrush calling through the fog
My daughter.   35

ISAAC ROSENBERG

Isaac Rosenberg was born of Jewish parents in Bristol on 25 November 1890. Seven years later his family moved to London, where he attended elementary schools in Stepney. He left school at the age of fourteen to become apprenticed as an engraver to a firm of art publishers. In the evenings he attended the Art School of Birkbeck College, for he wished to make painting his career. It was not until his apprenticeship was over that he was able to further his aims when he attended the Slade School, the means being provided for him by three ladies (Mrs Delissa Joseph, Miss E. D. Lowy and Mrs Herbert Cohen).

When he was very young he started to write poems, and he continued to write poetry while he studied painting at the Slade. His poems were privately printed in small printing houses in Stepney and Mile End. These pamphlets were privately circulated, and won Rosenberg modest acclaim. Like his painting, his poetry brought him little money.

When he was twenty-four he made a visit to South Africa, where his sister lived, in the hope that the climate would be beneficial to his lungs. He returned to England in 1915. He enlisted in the army, was sent out to France the next year and, after two years' active service at the front, he was killed on 1 April 1918.

FURTHER READING

Harding, D. W. 'The Poetry of Isaac Rosenberg'. *Scrutiny*, III. Cambridge, 1935.

Break of Day in the Trenches

The darkness crumbles away—
It is the same old druid Time as ever.
Only a live thing leaps my hand—
A queer sardonic rat—
As I pull the parapet's poppy   5
To stick behind my ear.
Droll rat, they would shoot you if they knew
Your cosmopolitan sympathies.

Now you have touched this English hand
You will do the same to a German—   10
Soon, no doubt, if it be your pleasure
To cross the sleeping green between.
It seems you inwardly grin as you pass
Strong eyes, fine limbs, haughty athletes
Less chanced than you for life,   15
Bonds to the whims of murder,
Sprawled in the bowels of the earth,
The torn fields of France.
What do you see in our eyes
At the shrieking iron and flame   20
Hurled through still heavens?
What quaver—what heart aghast?
Poppies whose roots are in man's veins
Drop, and are ever dropping;
But mine in my ear is safe,   25
Just a little white with the dust.

Returning, We Hear the Larks

Sombre the night is.
And though we have our lives, we know
What sinister threat lurks there.

Dragging these anguished limbs, we only know
This poison-blasted track opens on our camp—   5
On a little safe sleep.

But hark! joy—joy—strange joy.
Lo! heights of night ringing with unseen larks.
Music showering on our upturned list'ning faces.

Death could drop from the dark   10
As easily as song—
But song only dropped,
Like a blind man's dreams on the sand
By dangerous tides,
Like a girl's dark hair for she dreams no ruin lies there,   15
Or her kisses where a serpent hides.

Dead Man's Dump

The plunging limbers over the shattered track
Racketed with their rusty freight,
Stuck out like many crowns of thorns,
And the rusty stakes like sceptres old
To stay the flood of brutish men   5
Upon our brothers dear.

The wheels lurched over sprawled dead
But pained them not, though their bones crunched,
Their shut mouths made no moan.
They lie there huddled, friend and foeman,   10
Man born of man, and born of woman,
And shells go crying over them
From night till night and now.

Earth has waited for them,
All the time of their growth   15
Fretting for their decay:
Now she has them at last!
In the strength of their strength
Suspended—stopped and held.

What fierce imaginings their dark souls lit?   20
Earth! have they gone into you!
Somewhere they must have gone,
And flung on your hard back
Is their soul's sack
Emptied of God-ancestralled essences.   25
Who hurled them out? Who hurled?

None saw their spirits' shadow shake the grass,
Or stood aside for the half used life to pass
Out of those doomed nostrils and the doomed mouth,
When the swift iron burning bee   30
Drained the wild honey of their youth.

What of us who, flung on the shrieking pyre,
Walk, our usual thoughts untouched,
Our lucky limbs as on ichor fed,
Immortal seeming ever?   35

Perhaps when the flames beat loud on us,
A fear may choke in our veins
And the startled blood may stop.

The air is loud with death,
The dark air spurts with fire,   40
The explosions ceaseless are.
Timelessly now, some minutes past,
These dead strode time with vigorous life,
Till the shrapnel called 'An end!'
But not to all. In bleeding pangs   45
Some borne on stretchers dreamed of home,
Dear things, war-blotted from their hearts.

Maniac Earth! howling and flying, your bowel
Seared by the jagged fire, the iron love,
The impetuous storm of savage love.   50
Dark Earth! dark Heavens! swinging in chemic smoke,
What dead are born when you kiss each soundless soul
With lightning and thunder from your mined heart,
Which man's self dug, and his blind fingers loosed?

A man's brains splattered on   55
A stretcher-bearer's face;
His shook shoulders slipped their load,
But when they bend to look again
The drowning soul was sunk too deep
For human tenderness.   60

They left this dead with the older dead,
Stretched at the cross roads.

Burnt black by strange decay
Their sinister faces lie,
The lid over each eye,   65
The grass and coloured clay
More motion have than they,
Joined to the great sunk silences.

Here is one not long dead;
His dark hearing caught our far wheels,   70
And the choked soul stretched weak hands
To reach the living word the far wheels said,

The blood-dazed intelligence beating for light,
Crying through the suspense of the far torturing wheels
Swift for the end to break   75
Or the wheels to break,
Cried as the tide of the world broke over his sight.

Will they come? Will they ever come?
Even as the mixed hoofs of the mules,
The quivering-bellied mules,   80
And the rushing wheels all mixed
With his tortured upturned sight.
So we crashed round the bend,
We heard his weak scream,
We heard his very last sound,   85
And our wheels grazed his dead face.

WILFRED OWEN

Wilfred Edward Salter Owen was born at Plas Wilmot, a house
a few miles on the English side of the Welsh border, near Oswes-
try, on 18 March 1893. His father was a railway official. His
mother had been brought up in an atmosphere that combined
Victorian comfort with a strict, uncompromising Calvinism.
The marriage, though in many ways a happy one, was not
altogether free from tension. Wilfred, the eldest of their four
children, was the one on whom the mother lavished her care and
affection and the tie between mother and son was the closest
family tie that he was to know.

His education began at the Birkenhead Institute, but in 1907,
when Wilfred was fourteen, his father was moved to Shrewsbury.
The boy's education was continued at Shrewsbury Technical
School. In September 1911 he matriculated at London University. He had hoped for a university education but, as this was
impossible on his father's meagre financial resources, he went
as a pupil and lay assistant to the Reverend Herbert Wigan,
the Vicar of Dunsden, Oxfordshire. The possibility that Owen
might enter Holy Orders gradually evaporated as his faith in
Christian dogma and practice collapsed in the light of his social
experience. His lapse in faith together with a serious illness
brought his job at Dunsden to a close.

In August 1913 Owen took a poorly paid post at the Berlitz
School of Languages in Bordeaux, a post he held until July
1914 when he became a tutor to two boys in a Catholic family
in Bordeaux. A month later he was introduced to M. Laurent
Tailhade, a professional poet with strong pacifist convictions
who encouraged Owen to fulfil his poet's vocation.

In 1915 he returned from Bordeaux, enlisted in the Artists'
Rifles in October and was commissioned in the Manchester
Regiment in June 1916. After the Somme battles, Owen was
invalided to Craiglockhart War Hospital suffering from neuras-
thenia, caused, he said, by 'living so long by the *disiecta membra*
of a friend'.

It was while he was at Craiglockhart that Owen met Siegfried
Sassoon, already established as a war poet, whose poetry and
pacifism Owen found wholly congenial. Sassoon's encourage-

ment and criticism were immensely valued by Owen; so, too, was the friendship that Owen made with Sassoon and Osbert Sitwell. After a period of recuperation Owen returned to the western front, convinced that his protest against the horror of war would be the stronger if it was made from the position of the fighting man. He was awarded the Military Cross in October 1918. On 4 November 1918 he was killed by machine-gun fire while trying to get his men across the Sambre Canal.

The Preface to Owen's intended book of poems is as follows:

This book is not about heroes. English poetry is not yet fit to speak of them.

Nor is it about deeds, or lands, nor anything about glory, honour, might, majesty, dominion, or power, except War.

Above all I am not concerned with Poetry.

My subject is War, and the pity of War.

The Poetry is in the pity.

Yet these elegies are to this generation in no sense consolatory. They may be to the next. All a poet can do today is warn. That is why the true Poets must be truthful.

(If I thought the letter of this book would last, I might have used proper names; but if the spirit of it survives—survives Prussia—my ambition and those names will have achieved themselves fresher fields than Flanders...)

FURTHER READING: BIOGRAPHICAL WORKS

Owen, Harold. *Journey from Obscurity: Wilfred Owen, 1893–1919.* 3 vols., Oxford University Press, 1963–5.
Sassoon, Siegfried. *Siegfried's Journey.* Faber and Faber, 1945.
Sitwell, Sir Osbert. *Noble Essences.* Macmillan, 1950.

CRITICAL WORKS

Day Lewis, C. (ed., and with notes and introduction; and Memoir by Edmund Blunden). *The Collected Poems of Wilfred Owen.* Chatto and Windus, 1964.
Welland, D. S. R. *Wilfred Owen: a Critical Study.* Chatto and Windus, 1960.

Strange Meeting

It seemed that out of battle I escaped
Down some profound dull tunnel, long since scooped
Through granites which titanic wars had groined.
Yet also there encumbered sleepers groaned,
Too fast in thought or death to be bestirred.   5
Then, as I probed them, one sprang up, and stared
With piteous recognition in fixed eyes,
Lifting distressful hands as if to bless.
And by his smile, I knew that sullen hall,
By his dead smile I knew we stood in Hell.   10
With a thousand pains that vision's face was grained;
Yet no blood reached there from the upper ground,
And no guns thumped, or down the flues made moan.
'Strange friend,' I said, 'here is no cause to mourn.'
'None,' said that other, 'save the undone years,   15
The hopelessness. Whatever hope is yours,
Was my life also; I went hunting wild
After the wildest beauty in the world,
Which lies not calm in eyes, or braided hair,
But mocks the steady running of the hour,   20
And if it grieves, grieves richlier than here.
For of my glee might many men have laughed,
And of my weeping something had been left,
Which must die now. I mean the truth untold,
The pity of war, the pity war distilled.   25
Now men will go content with what we spoiled,
Or, discontent, boil bloody, and be spilled.
They will be swift with swiftness of the tigress.
None will break ranks, though nations trek from progress.
Courage was mine, and I had mystery,   30
Wisdom was mine, and I had mastery;
To miss the march of this retreating world
Into vain citadels that are not walled.
Then, when much blood had clogged their chariot-wheels,
I would go up and wash them from sweet wells,   35
Even with truths that lie too deep for taint.
I would have poured my spirit without stint
But not through wounds; not on the cess of war.

Foreheads of men have bled where no wounds were.
I am the enemy you killed, my friend.   40
I knew you in this dark: for so you frowned
Yesterday through me as you jabbed and killed.
I parried; but my hands were loath and cold.
Let us sleep now...'

Anthem for Doomed Youth

What passing bells for these who die as cattle?
    Only the monstrous anger of the guns.
    Only the stuttering rifles' rapid rattle
Can patter out their hasty orisons.
No mockeries now for them; no prayers nor bells,   5
    Nor any voice of mourning save the choirs,—
The shrill, demented choirs of wailing shells;
    And bugles calling for them from sad shires.

What candles may be held to speed them all?
    Not in the hands of boys, but in their eyes   10
Shall shine the holy glimmers of good-byes.
    The pallor of girls' brows shall be their pall;
Their flowers the tenderness of patient minds,
And each slow dusk a drawing-down of blinds.

The Send-off

Down the close, darkening lanes they sang their way
To the siding-shed,
And lined the train with faces grimly gay.

Their breasts were stuck all white with wreath and spray
As men's are, dead.   5

Dull porters watched them, and a casual tramp
Stood staring hard,
Sorry to miss them from the upland camp,
Then, unmoved, signals nodded, and a lamp
Winked to the guard.   10

So secretly, like wrongs hushed-up, they went.
They were not ours:
We never heard to which front these were sent.

Nor there if they yet mock what women meant
Who gave them flowers.   15

Shall they return to beatings of great bells
In wild train-loads?
A few, a few, too few for drums and yells,
May creep back, silent, to still village wells
Up half-known roads.   20

Exposure

Our brains ache, in the merciless iced east winds that knive
    us...
Wearied we keep awake because the night is silent...
Low, drooping flares confuse our memory of the salient...
Worried by silence, sentries whisper, curious, nervous,
    But nothing happens.   5

Watching, we hear the mad gusts tugging on the wire,
Like twitching agonies of men among its brambles.
Northward, incessantly, the flickering gunnery rumbles,
Far off, like a dull rumour of some other war.
    What are we doing here?   10

The poignant misery of dawn begins to grow...
We only know war lasts, rain soaks, and clouds sag stormy.
Dawn massing in the east her melancholy army
Attacks once more in ranks on shivering ranks of gray,
    But nothing happens.   15

Sudden successive flights of bullets streak the silence.
Less deathly than the air that shudders black with snow,
With sidelong flowing flakes that flock, pause, and renew;
We watch them wandering up and down the wind's
    nonchalance,
    But nothing happens.   20

Pale flakes with fingering stealth come feeling for our faces—
We cringe in holes, back on forgotten dreams, and stare,
    snow-dazed,
Deep into grassier ditches. So we drowse, sun-dozed,
Littered with blossoms trickling where the blackbird fusses.
    Is it that we are dying?   25

Slowly our ghosts drag home: glimpsing the sunk fires, glozed
With crusted dark-red jewels; crickets jingle there;
For hours the innocent mice rejoice: the house is theirs;
Shutters and doors, all closed: on us the doors are closed,—
    We turn back to our dying. 30

Since we believe not otherwise can kind fires burn;
Nor ever suns smile true on child, or field, or fruit.
For God's invincible spring our love is made afraid;
Therefore, not loath, we lie out here; therefore were born,
    For love of God seems dying. 35

To-night, His frost will fasten on this mud and us,
Shrivelling many hands, puckering foreheads crisp.
The burying-party, picks and shovels in their shaking grasp,
Pause over half-known faces. All their eyes are ice,
    But nothing happens. 40

Futility

Move him into the sun—
Gently its touch awoke him once,
At home, whispering of fields unsown.
Always it woke him, even in France,
Until this morning and this snow. 5
If anything might rouse him now
The kind old sun will know.

Think how it wakes the seeds,—
Woke, once, the clays of a cold star.
Are limbs, so dear-achieved, are sides, 10
Full-nerved—still warm—too hard to stir?
Was it for this the clay grew tall?
—O what made fatuous sunbeams toil
To break earth's sleep at all?

Mental Cases

Who are these? Why sit they here in twilight?
Wherefore rock they, purgatorial shadows,
Drooping tongues from jaws that slob their relish,
Baring teeth that leer like skull's teeth wicked?

Stroke on stroke of pain,—but what slow panic,   5
Gouged these chasms round their fretted sockets?
Ever from their hair and through their hands' palms
Misery swelters. Surely we have perished
Sleeping, and walk hell; but who these hellish?

—These are men whose minds the Dead have ravished.   10
Memory fingers in their hair of murders,
Multitudinous murders they once witnessed.
Wading sloughs of flesh these helpless wander,
Treading blood from lungs that had loved laughter.
Always they must see these things and hear them,   15
Batter of guns and shatter of flying muscles,
Carnage incomparable, and human squander
Rucked too thick for these men's extrication.

Therefore still their eyeballs shrink tormented
Back into their brains, because on their sense   20
Sunlight seems a blood-smear; night comes blood-black;
Dawn breaks open like a wound that bleeds afresh,
—Thus their heads wear this hilarious, hideous,
Awful falseness of set-smiling corpses.
—Thus their hands are plucking at each other;   25
Picking at the rope-knouts of their scourging;
Snatching after us who smote them, brother,
Pawing us who dealt them war and madness.

Miners

There was a whispering in my hearth,
    A sigh of the coal,
Grown wistful of a former earth
    It might recall.

I listened for a tale of leaves   5
    And smothered ferns;
Frond-forests; and the low, sly lives
    Before the fawns.

My fire might show steam-phantoms simmer
    From Time's old cauldron,
Before the birds made nests in summer,   10
    Or men had children.

But the coals were murmuring of their mine,
    And moans down there
Of boys that slept wry sleep, and men   15
    Writhing for air.

And I saw white bones in the cinder-shard.
    Bones without number;
For many hearts with coal are charred
    And few remember.   20

I thought of some who worked dark pits
    Of war, and died
Digging the rock where Death reputes
    Peace lies indeed.

Comforted years will sit soft-chaired   25
    In rooms of amber;
The years will stretch their hands, well-cheered
    By our lives' ember.

The centuries will burn rich loads
    With which we groaned,   30
Whose warmth shall lull their dreaming lids
    While songs are crooned.
But they will not dream of us poor lads
    Lost in the ground.

W.H.AUDEN

W. H. Auden was born in York in 1907, the son of a doctor.
Educated first at a public school, he subsequently went up to
Oxford where, as an undergraduate at Christ Church, he established a considerable reputation as a poet. After some time in
Germany, before the advent of Hitler, he returned to England
and became, briefly, a schoolmaster. More significantly, he
became the principal figure in the literary movement of the
1930s which first brought to public attention the work of a
group of poets, comprising among others Stephen Spender,
C. Day Lewis, and Louis MacNeice, with the publication in
1932 of an anthology entitled *New Signatures*. They were deeply
committed to diagnosing the political and social malaise of their
time; Auden mirrors in his work, and in the plays he wrote in
collaboration with Christopher Isherwood, most of their dominant concerns. He went to Spain in 1937, during the Spanish
Civil War, and left England, finally, for the United States of
America in 1938. The poems here chosen to represent his work
were all written prior to 1939, and show the diversity of his
concern with both social man and his landscape. His was the most
considerable talent in this generation of poets.

FURTHER READING

Blair, J. G. *The Poetic Art of W. H. Auden.* Oxford University Press, 1967. 821.91
Fuller, John. *A Reader's Guide to W. H. Auden.* Thames and Hudson, 1970. 821.91
Hoggart, Richard. *Auden: an Introductory Essay.* Chatto and Windus, 1951. 821.91
Spears, Monroe K. *The Poetry of W. H. Auden.* O.U.P., 1963. 821.91

The Watershed

Who stands, the crux left of the watershed,
On the wet road between the chafing grass
Below him sees dismantled washing-floors,
Snatches of tramline running to a wood,
An industry already comatose,   5
Yet sparsely living. A ramshackle engine
At Cashwell raises water; for ten years
It lay in flooded workings until this,
Its latter office, grudgingly performed.

[127]

And, further, here and there, though many dead   10
Lie under the poor soil, some acts are chosen
Taken from recent winters; two there were
Cleaned out a damaged shaft by hand, clutching
The winch a gale would tear them from; one died
During a storm, the fells impassable,   15
Not at his village, but in wooden shape
Through long abandoned levels nosed his way
And in his final valley went to ground.

Go home, now, stranger, proud of your young stock,
Stranger, turn back again, frustrate and vexed: 20
This land, cut off, will not communicate,
Be no accessory content to one
Aimless for faces rather there than here.
Beams from your car may cross a bedroom wall,
They wake no sleeper; you may hear the wind   25
Arriving driven from the ignorant sea
To hurt itself on pane, on bark of elm
Where sap unbaffled rises, being spring;
But seldom this. Near you, taller than grass,
Ears poise before decision, scenting danger.   30

In Memory of W. B. Yeats
(*d. Jan. 1939*)

I

He disappeared in the dead of winter:
The brooks were frozen, the airports almost deserted,
And snow disfigured the public statues;
The mercury sank in the mouth of the dying day.
What instruments we have agree   5
The day of his death was a dark cold day.

Far from his illness
The wolves ran on through the evergreen forests,
The peasant river was untempted by the fashionable quays;
By mourning tongues   10
The death of the poet was kept from his poems.

But for him it was his last afternoon as himself,
An afternoon of nurses and rumours;

The provinces of his body revolted,
The squares of his mind were empty,   15
Silence invaded the suburbs,
The current of his feeling failed; he became his admirers.

Now he is scattered among a hundred cities
And wholly given over to unfamiliar affections,
To find his happiness in another kind of wood   20
And be punished under a foreign code of conscience.
The words of a dead man
Are modified in the guts of the living.

But in the importance and noise of to-morrow
When the brokers are roaring like beasts on the floor of the
        Bourse,   25
And the poor have the sufferings to which they are fairly
        accustomed,
And each in the cell of himself is almost convinced of his
        freedom,
A few thousand will think of this day
As one thinks of a day when one did something slightly
        unusual.
What instruments we have agree   30
The day of his death was a dark cold day.

II

You were silly like us; your gift survived it all:
The parish of rich women, physical decay,
Yourself. Mad Ireland hurt you into poetry.
Now Ireland has her madness and her weather still,   35
For poetry makes nothing happen: it survives
In the valley of its making where executives
Would never want to tamper, flows on south
From ranches of isolation and the busy griefs,
Raw towns that we believe and die in; it survives,   40
A way of happening, a mouth.

III

Earth, receive an honoured guest:
William Yeats is laid to rest.
Let the Irish vessel lie
Emptied of its poetry.   45

In the nightmare of the dark
All the dogs of Europe bark,
And the living nations wait,
Each sequestered in its hate;

Intellectual disgrace   50
Stares from every human face,
And the seas of pity lie
Locked and frozen in each eye.

Follow, poet, follow right
To the bottom of the night,   55
With your unconstraining voice
Still persuade us to rejoice;

With the farming of a verse
Make a vineyard of the curse,
Sing of human unsuccess   60
In a rapture of distress;

In the deserts of the heart
Let the healing fountain start,
In the prison of his days
Teach the free man how to praise.   65

O What is that Sound

O what is that sound which so thrills the ear
  Down in the valley drumming, drumming?
Only the scarlet soldiers, dear,
  The soldiers coming.

O what is that light I see flashing so clear   5
  Over the distance brightly, brightly?
Only the sun on their weapons, dear,
  As they step lightly.

O what are they doing with all that gear,
  What are they doing this morning, this morning?   10
Only their usual manoeuvres, dear,
  Or perhaps a warning.

O why have they left the road down there,
  Why are they suddenly wheeling, wheeling?

Perhaps a change in their orders, dear.   15
    Why are you kneeling?

O haven't they stopped for the doctor's care,
    Haven't they reined their horses, their horses?
Why, they are none of them wounded, dear,
    None of these forces.   20

O is it the parson they want, with white hair,
    Is it the parson, is it, is it?
No, they are passing his gateway, dear,
    Without a visit.

O it must be the farmer who lives so near.   25
    It must be the farmer so cunning, so cunning?
They have passed the farmyard already, dear,
    And now they are running.

O where are you going? Stay with me here!
    Were the vows you swore deceiving, deceiving?   30
No, I promised to love you, dear,
    But I must be leaving.

O it's broken the lock and splintered the door,
    O it's the gate where they're turning, turning;
Their boots are heavy on the floor   35
    And their eyes are burning.

On This Island

Look, stranger, on this island now
The leaping light for your delight discovers,
Stand stable here
And silent be,
That through the channels of the ear   5
May wander like a river
The swaying sound of the sea.

Here at the small field's ending pause
When the chalk wall falls to the foam and its tall ledges
Oppose the pluck   10
And knock of the tide,
And the shingle scrambles after the suck-
-ing surf,
And the gull lodges
A moment on its sheer side.   15

Far off like floating seeds the ships
Diverge on urgent voluntary errands,
And the full view
Indeed may enter
And move in memory as now these clouds do,   20
That pass the harbour mirror
And all the summer through the water saunter.

Edward Lear

Left by his friend to breakfast alone on the white
Italian shore, his Terrible Demon arose
Over his shoulder; he wept to himself in the night,
A dirty landscape-painter who hated his nose.

The legions of cruel inquisitive They   5
Were so many and big like dogs: he was upset
By Germans and boats; affection was miles away:
But guided by tears he successfully reached his Regret.

How prodigious the welcome was. Flowers took his hat
And bore him off to introduce him to the tongs;   10
The demon's false nose made the table laugh; a cat
Soon had him waltzing madly, let him squeeze her hand;
Words pushed him to the piano to sing comic songs;

And children swarmed to him like settlers. He became a land.

Musée des Beaux Arts

About suffering they were never wrong,
The Old Masters: how well they understood
Its human position; how it takes place
While someone else is eating or opening a window or just
        walking dully along;
How, when the aged are reverently, passionately waiting   5
For the miraculous birth, there always must be
Children who did not specially want it to happen, skating
On a pond at the edge of the wood:
They never forgot
That even the dreadful martyrdom must run its course   10
Anyhow in a corner, some untidy spot

Where the dogs go on with their doggy life and the
    torturer's horse
Scratches its innocent behind on a tree.

In Brueghel's *Icarus*, for instance: how everything turns away
Quite leisurely from the disaster; the ploughman may   15
Have heard the splash, the forsaken cry,
But for him it was not an important failure; the sun shone
As it had to on the white legs disappearing into the green
Water; and the expensive delicate ship that must have seen
Something amazing, a boy falling out of the sky,   20
Had somewhere to get to and sailed calmly on.

A Summer Night

(*To Geoffrey Hoyland*)

Out on the lawn I lie in bed,
Vega conspicuous overhead
   In the windless nights of June,
As congregated leaves complete
Their day's activity; my feet   5
   Point to the rising moon.

Lucky, this point in time and space
Is chosen as my working-place,
   Where the sexy airs of summer,
The bathing hours and the bare arms,   10
The leisured drives through a land of farms
   Are good to a newcomer.

Equal with colleagues in a ring
I sit on each calm evening
   Enchanted as the flowers   15
The opening light draws out of hiding
With all its gradual dove-like pleading,
   Its logic and its powers:

That later we, though parted then,
May still recall these evenings when   20
   Fear gave his watch no look;
The lion griefs loped from the shade
And on our knees their muzzle laid,
   And Death put down his book.

Now north and south and east and west   25
Those I love lie down to rest;
  The moon looks on them all,
The healers and the brilliant talkers
The eccentrics and the silent walkers,
  The dumpy and the tall.   30

She climbs the European sky,
Churches and power-stations lie
  Alike among earth's fixtures:
Into the galleries she peers
And blankly as a butcher stares   35
  Upon the marvellous pictures.

To gravity attentive, she
Can notice nothing here, though we
  Whom hunger does not move,
From gardens where we feel secure   40
Look up and with a sigh endure
  The tyrannies of love:

And, gentle, do not care to know,
Where Poland draws her eastern bow,
  What violence is done,   45
Nor ask what doubtful act allows
Our freedom in this English house,
  Our picnics in the sun.

Soon, soon, through dykes of our content
The crumpling flood will force a rent   50
  And, taller than a tree,
Hold sudden death before our eyes
Whose river dreams long hid the size
  And vigours of the sea.

But when the waters make retreat   55
And through the black mud first the wheat
  In shy green stalks appears,
When stranded monsters gasping lie,
And sounds of riveting terrify
  Their whorled unsubtle ears,   60

May these delights we dread to lose,
This privacy, need no excuse

But to that strength belong,
As through a child's rash happy cries
The drowned parental voices rise   65
    In unlamenting song.

After discharges of alarm
All unpredicted let them calm
    The pulse of nervous nations,
Forgive the murderer in his glass,   70
Tough in their patience to surpass
    The tigress her swift motions.

The Unknown Citizen

*(To JS/07/M/378 This Marble Monument
Is Erected to the State)*

He was found by the Bureau of Statistics to be
One against whom there was no official complaint,
And all the reports on his conduct agree
That, in the modern sense of an old-fashioned word, he was
    a saint,
For in everything he did he served the Greater Community.   5
Except for the War till the day he retired
He worked in a factory and never got fired,
But satisfied his employers, Fudge Motors Inc.
Yet he wasn't a scab or odd in his views,
For his Union reports that he paid his dues,   10
(Our report on his Union shows it was sound)
And our Social Psychology workers found
That he was popular with his mates and liked a drink.
The Press are convinced that he bought a paper every day
And that his reactions to advertisements were normal in every
    way.   15
Policies taken out in his name prove that he was fully insured,
And his Health-card shows he was once in hospital but left it
    cured.
Both Producers Research and High-Grade Living declare
He was fully sensible to the advantages of the Instalment
    Plan
And had everything necessary to the Modern Man,   20
A phonograph, a radio, a car and a frigidaire.

Our researchers into Public Opinion are content
That he held the proper opinions for the time of year;
When there was peace, he was for peace; when there was war,
    he went.
He was married and added five children to the population,   25
Which our Eugenist says was the right number for a parent
    of his generation,
And our teachers report that he never interfered with their
    education.
Was he free? Was he happy? The question is absurd:
Had anything been wrong, we should certainly have heard.

NOTES TO THE POEMS

GERARD MANLEY
HOPKINS

Winter with the Gulf Stream

This poem was published in a periodical, *Once a Week*, 14 February 1863. Hopkins told Bridges that the poem had been written at Highgate School. Bridges conjectured that Hopkins had revised the poem since. It is included in this selection to illustrate Hopkins' keen response to the physical world at the outset of his poetic career.

15] *bugle moon:* horn-shaped.
17] *a berg of hyaline:* iceberg of crystal.
26] *beryl-covered:* pale bluish-green (a beryl is a precious stone belonging to the same mineral species as an emerald).
27] *Pactolus:* the golden river which healed King Midas.
28] *brindled:* streaked.

The Habit of Perfection

This poem was written in 1866, the year of Hopkins' conversion to Roman Catholicism. The earlier version of two that exist was subtitled 'The Novice'. The poem is eloquent of Hopkins' desire to deny the bodily senses in order to come nearer to spiritual perfection, and makes its point by a paradoxical effect; the senses are rejected in a sensuous and physical exploration in poetic terms of their very nature and inwardness. The even unassertive tone plays against the cost of what is known, valued and, for the sake of a greater perfection, denied.

1] *Elected:* chosen as a means of salvation.
2] *whorlèd:* curled and convoluted like a shell.
6] *shut:* the silencing, the closing of 'lovely-dumb' lips.
9] *shellèd:* closed with the eyelids. The sense of hardness suggested by 'shellèd' makes the eyelids a kind of carapace, though so delicate is the word that the loveliness of contour of the closed eye is equally felt.
10] *the uncreated light:* 'the creative energy of God's mind' (Gardner).
11–12] *ruck and reel:* these two nouns convey the crowded turbulence of the world, the vortex of material things, which distract the mind. The three verbs 'Coils, keeps, and teases' physically enact the way that the mind is confused, seized hold of and distracted by the pressure of material objects seen and hankered after.
13] *hutch:* the place of storing. The complex of thick *u*'s and consonants makes concrete the nature of the sense of taste.
15] *the can:* vessel for drinking.

18] *the stir and keep:* the excitement and upkeep. 'Keep' may also carry the meaning of a stronghold, a tower.

24] *And you unhouse and house the Lord:* and you, hands, shall offer the holy sacraments at the celebration of the Mass.

28] See Matt. vi. 28–9: 'Behold the lilies of the field, they toil not neither do they spin...'

God's Grandeur

Hopkins gives a clue to the interpretation of this poem and 'The Starlight Night' in a note written shortly after the poems' composition in early 1877. 'To be read, both of them, slowly, strongly marking the rhythms and fetching out the syllables.' Read aloud thus, the outbursting power and magnificence of the opening four lines contrast with the weighted exhaustion of the succeeding lines of the octave. The sestet registers a resurgence of a felt beneficent presence.

1] Cf. Hopkins' Sermons: 'All things therefore are charged with love, are charged with God and if we know how to touch them, give off sparks and take fire, yield drops and flow, ring and tell of him.'

2] *shook foil:* in a letter Hopkins writes: 'I mean foil in its sense of leaf or tinsel...Shaken gold foil gives off broad glares like sheet lightning, and also, and this is true of nothing else, owing to its zigzag dints and creasings and network of small many cornered facets, a sort of fork lightning too.'

The flash of the 'shook foil' is linked to the verb 'charged' in the preceding line, the force and concreteness of the simile giving warrant to the verb's dynamic suggestiveness. 'Charged' carries both its sense of 'filled to the brim', as well as its 'electrical' overtones.

3] The alliteration of 'gathers to a greatness' links with the phrase 'grandeur of God' in line 1, echoing it. But instead of the blaze, the simile is softened in vowel sound and sensuous richness with 'ooze of oil / Crushed.'

5–8] The awareness of a world de-natured by man's actions and work is conveyed as powerfully by the rhythmic stress and the clogging internal rhymes as by the meaning of the words.

9 et seq.] The plenitude of God's grandeur is asserted in tenderness and colour. The light 'springing' in the East supersedes the stain of the world and its work in 'bleared, smeared...smudge'.

13] Cf. Gen. i. 2: 'And the earth was without form, and void; and darkness was upon the face of the deep. And the Spirit of God moved upon the face of the waters' and *Paradise Lost*, book 1, lines 19–22:

> 'Thou from the first
> Wast present, and with mighty wings outspread
> Dove-like satst brooding on the vast Abyss
> And mad'st it pregnant.'

The Starlight Night

The ecstatic contemplation of the night sky, the feeling of 'this wonder here, now' is communicated in exclamations of joy and explosions of metaphor rapidly and richly succeeding one another. Pace combines with fabulous suggestiveness to create afresh the experience of starlight. The stars mark the boundaries of Christ's home.

4] *delves:* mines.

6] *wind-beat whitebeam:* the leaves of the whitebeam have silvery undersides which swing uppermost when the tree is blown by the wind.

abeles: a species of poplar.

8] *a purchase, all is a prize:* understanding of the beauty of the universe has to be paid for by 'Prayer, patience, alms, vows'. This asceticism and self-denial gives place to an ecstasy of beholding in lines 10 and 11.

12] *barn:* Matt. xiii. 30: '...gather the wheat into my barn.'

13] *shocks:* stooks (of corn).

piece-bright paling: the hurdles of the stars around the barn of Christ.

14] *his hallows:* his saints.

The Windhover: To Christ our Lord

In a letter to Bridges of 22 June 1879, Hopkins promised to send him an amended copy of 'The Windhover' and added that it 'is the best thing I ever wrote'. His assessment has been endorsed since by critics, despite their varying interpretation of it.

1] *minion:* favourite, darling.

2] *dauphin:* literally the King of France's eldest son, but the meaning here is clearly of Christ the Son of God, the King of Heaven, of Light.

dapple-dawn-drawn: the spots and lines of reddish-brown colour on the falcon; or the falcon drawn against the dappled sky of dawn.

Falcon: The capital F limits the metaphor to the bird/Christ identi-fication.

3-4] The sense of gliding poise in the bird's flight is dramatically contrasted with the soaring upward movement enacted in the striding turn of the bird.

4] *High there:* where the voice stresses 'high' and maintains it on 'there'.

how he rung upon the rein of a wimpling wing: 'rung upon the rein' is a term from horsemanship, the horse circling upon a long rein, held by its trainer. 'rung' is also a term from falconry, meaning to soar upwards in spirals. 'wimpling': W. H. Gardner notes how this word combines the static sense of 'beautifully curved, and pleated quill over quill' with the dynamic sense of 'swinging, fluttering'.

5-7] The mimetic effect of the rhythm here is exceptionally powerful: syntax, alliteration and onomatopoeia work together.

7-8] Hopkins' sense of his own impotence and lack of achievement ('my heart in hiding') gives place to wonder and awe (the ecstatic gasp at the comma 'the achieve of,') and maybe a sense of the possibility of participating in this bird's 'heroic graces'.

9-14] The sestet develops 'the achieve of, the mastery of the thing' in minute dynamic particulars, embodying in the texture and movement and maximum suggestiveness of the poetry the nature of the bird/Christ's mastery and achievement. Hopkins wrote: 'I *inscape* this windhover as the symbol or analogue of Christ, Son of God, the supreme Chevalier. May the human equivalents of the bird's heroic graces and perfectly disciplined *physical* activity be combined and brought to a much higher *spiritual* activity in my own being, just as these attributes were once and for all so transmuted in Christ.'

9] The interweaving of abstract and concrete nouns, each empowered to

work like interjections of admiration, gather together on 'here' for the heavily
accented word 'Buckle' (line 10). Both words ('here / Buckle') carry an
ambiguity of meaning which, although making for interpretative difficulties,
gives poetic richness to the sestet.

here: either 'here in my heart, in me': or 'in this bird, at this moment'.
10] *Buckle:* the mood of this verb and its meaning have perplexed many
critics. Buckle can have three meanings: (1) collapse, give way under stress
crumple. This meaning is viable if the verb is indicative. Buckle can also
mean (2) come to grips, prepare for action, or (3) clasp, enclose or fasten
together, if the verb is to be understood as being imperative (Hopkins is thus
addressing himself (his 'heart in hiding') which may achieve the Falcon/
Christ's beauty and grace. The gist of the sestet is that the heart prepared for
sacrifice and suffering comes nearest to the beauty of Christ's sacrifice of
Himself; Christ's 'failure' is paradoxically the condition and moment of
this triumph, cf. Hopkins' Sermons: 'Christ our Lord was doomed to
succeed by failure; his plans were baffled, his hopes dashed and his work done
by being broken off undone...'
11] *O my Chevalier:* apostrophe to Christ. 'Chevalier' carries with it the
meanings of knight, rider (thus linking the sestet with horseriding imagery in
the octave).
12] The turning of the earth with the ploughshare makes it gleam and shine.
    sillion: strip of arable, furrow.
13] Grey, apparently cold, embers glow red-hot and golden as they fall and
break open.
    ah my dear: an address to Christ.

The Lantern out of Doors

Christ's abiding love for and concern over the lot of each individual is
contrasted with the fallibility of human 'interest' in other people:

'...till death or distance buys them quite.
Death or distance soon consumes them:...'

4] *wading:* moving with the invisible stride of the carrier, and swaying.
9-10] *wind | What most I may eye after:* Dr Gardner points out that the
verb is 'wind eye after' and quotes Hopkins: 'I mean that the eye winds /
only in the sense that its focus or point of sight winds and that coincides with a
point of the object and winds with that. For the object, a lantern passing
further and further away and bearing now east, now west of one right line,
is truly and properly described as winding.'

The Candle Indoors

A companion piece to 'The Lantern out of Doors': both spring from the
sight of a light shining within the darkness. Here the actual (either real or
vividly imagined) occasion of the candlelight shining through the window is
linked with the following passage from Matt. v. 13-16:
'Ye are the salt of the earth: but if the salt have lost his savour, wherewith
shall it be salted? It is therefore good for nothing, but to be cast out and to
be trodden under foot of men.
    Ye are the light of the world. A city that is set on a hill cannot be hid.

Neither do men light a candle and put it under a bushel but on a candle-
stick; and it giveth light unto all that are in the house.

Let your light so shine before men that they may see your good works,
and glorify your Father which is in heaven.'

Significantly Hopkins is outside the house; cut off, as it were, from the
warmth and fulfilment of tasks undertaken by the Jessys and Jacks of this
world and their attendant satisfactions. Hence the note of longing in the
opening of the sestet.

4] *to-fro tender trambeams truckle at the eye:* as the eyelids of the watcher
move ever so slightly backwards and forwards the eyelashes cause delicate
beams of light, like fine silken threads, to radiate from the candle's flame.

Silk threads used for the weft of the best silk goods are called 'trams'. It is
also possible that trambeams could refer to the flash of light on the metal
rails on which tramcars used to run.

truckle at: wince at a blow, quail at the sight; or in the sense of truckling to
a person—a kind of flattery.

8] *There /:* the oblique stroke indicates a pause. So the voice falls on 'There'
and again on 'God'. thus emphasising the moment in Time and the Being
that transcends Time.

aggrándize: magnify.

9] *Come you indoors:* the poet addresses himself in the last six lines of the
poem: i.e. confront the personal situation within yourself.

Felix Randal

This poem was written in April 1880 when Hopkins was working in Liverpool. Hopkins uses Lancashire dialect here ('and all'; 'all road ever'). The
colloquial opening with its tone of compassion in both the enquiry and the
confirmation is the occasion for a meditation on the nature of Hopkins'
priestly duties and their effect upon him.

1] *farrier:* blacksmith.
2] *his mould of man:* stature, build, expressed as an image from iron-
founding.
3] *time when reason rambled in it:* when his mind began to wander.
6] *and all:* Lancashire dialect; as well, in addition.
7] *our sweet reprieve and ransom:* Holy Communion.
8] *all road ever he offended* (Lancashire dialect): in whatever way he sinned.
9] This witnessing of the sick (and dying) stirs up our compassion and love
for them, makes us aware of their worth and in so doing adds to our own
worth.
10] The unembarrassing tenderness of Hopkins springs from his perception
of what the splendid physique of the farrier has now become in its present
helplessness.
13] *random:* either, 'thoughtless' or 'heedless', in contrast with the blacksmith's later mood, or an architectural term for the stonework of the forge.
14] *fettle:* Northern dialect; fashion.

As kingfishers catch fire...

Hopkins was deeply influenced by the writings of the medieval theologian
Duns Scotus 'who of all men most sways my spirit to peace'. Scotus taught

that all things by their natures (what Hopkins repeatedly referred to as their *selves*), are a manifestation of the rich variety of God's creative power. By attempting to arrive at an insight into each creature's or thing's especial nature, the essence of his being, we gain a fuller understanding of the nature of God. Man's nature is made manifest in its highest state of being in the Incarnation of Christ.

1] *catch fire...dráw fláme:* the metaphors in these analogies communicate the different *nature* of the flight of the kingfisher and the dragonfly (the former swift, darting; the latter hovering and slow) and show how each creature, acting according to his kind, generates its own especial fire. Note should be taken of the speed of the first four words and the slower drawn out quality of the stressed words 'dráw fláme'.

3] *tucked:* touched, but also curled over the peg.

  tells: sounds out.

3–4] *bell's | Bow:* the interior of the cup of a bell.

5] *Each mortal thing:* the colloquial phrase is refurbished with meaning in this setting.

7] *Selves:* expresses its own essential being.

9–10] *justices:* acts in a just way, vivified by God's grace in all his thoughts and deeds.

12–14] By the means of grace, man in all the variety of his being and behaviour may move towards attaining the perfect beauty of Incarnate Christ.

Spelt from Sibyl's Leaves

This is the first of Hopkins' sonnets written during his last years in Dublin. The poem explores the condition of the 'dark night of the soul' with a sweep of line and a resonant suggestiveness of image and rhythm. There is a lofty grandeur about its opening which, as the poem proceeds, becomes charged with menace and terror of the Judgement. Hopkins told Bridges in a letter (11 December 1886) that the poem was made 'for performance and that its performance is not reading with the eye but loud, leisurely, poetical (not rhetorical) recitation, with long rests, long dwells on the rhyme and other marked syllables and so on. This sonnet should be almost sung: it is most carefully timed in *tempo rubato*.' W. H. Gardner writes: 'Its style, with its clotted consonants, harsh staccato and brusque emphasis, makes it one of the hardest of all the poems to appreciate. To produce the best effect it should be spoken by several voices, like a Greek chorus, some parts in unison, others antiphonally.'

Title] *Spelt:* in the sense of interpreting a mystery.

  Sibyl: a reference to the Cumaean Sibyl, the prophetic votaress of the Greek god Apollo who conducted Aeneas into Avernus. Sibyl means 'will of God'.

  Leaves: of a book of prophecy; but also the leaves of line 9. By his reference to the Sibyl, Hopkins endows his poem with a depth in time that reaches back beyond Christianity to pagan antiquity.

1] The bell-beats of the epithets call up in the mind's eye a vision of the sky at evening.

  Earnest: suggests a quiet intensity of thought and attitude.

equal: the evening reduces the variety of things 'under the eye of day', levels out shape and colour, drains away colour.

attuneable: the fading light of the vast evening sky is harmonized with the soul of man.

vaulty: the vast shape of the evening sky is seen as a vault, a created form (a roof or tomb).

voluminous: enhances awareness of the vault's size and carries with it a sense of light in the concealed 'luminous', and of the terror of being enveloped in something constricting.

stupendous: the pause before this word gives time for the epithet to issue forth with the full suggestiveness and weight of the preceding six epithets.

2] *strains:* connotes energy and longing, and the pain of birth.

womb-of-all, home-of-all, hearse-of-all night: night becomes the symbol of the whole mystery of existence from conception to decease.

3] *Her fond yellow hornlight:* the first rays of the rising moon. The quality of the light is compared to the yellowish/orange glow in an old lant*horn*, and the shape of the moon with the musical horn.

hoarlight: the light of the stars, like frost.

6] *throughther:* (dialect)—through one another.

páshed: beaten.

7] *Disremembering:* Irish dialect for 'forgetting'.

round: warn.

The sublime opening of the poem gives place in the last two lines of the octave to the menacing suggestion of ruin and dissolution. 'Páshed' heralds this with its sense of being beaten into loss of identity. The 'breakdown' is further enacted in the 'disremembering, dísmémbering' until selfhood is lost as it were, in a vast wave of darkness flooding irresistibly in 'whélms, whélms, ánd will end us'. It is significant how the stresses are marked in this line so that the emphasis falls upon the words that enact the triumphant power of the darkness.

9] *damask:* etched on the blade of a threatening sword (? of justice) (damascene work).

10] *Óur tale...!:* a prophecy which applies to us. 'Oracle' refers to the Cumaean Sibyl of the title.

11] *párt, pen, páck:* Let life herd everything into two flocks, separate the sheep from the goats, the wrong from the right.

14] *sheathe-and shelterless:* without sheathe or shelter. The reader experiences the rawness of the pain occasioned by the self-questioning in the hindered movement of the words and the jostle and conflict of the consonants. The alliteration here does nothing to smooth out the sound of the words: rather it sharpens their edges.

(Carrion Comfort)

Though Hopkins finds himself a victim of a profound Despair, the sonnet (written in 1885) opens with a resolute rejection of this mood which, if given free rein, would lead to suicide. The sonnet explores the cause of the Despair (his feelings of abandonment by God for whom he has sacrificed everything), and defines the cost of his resolution. The opening 'Not, I'll not' has an aggressive force which is the poet's only way of countering the debilitating effect of his 'carrion comfort'.

5] *O thou terrible:* God.

rude: used as an adverb; violently, in a rough, uncouth manner.

6] *wring-world:* world-wringing.

6–8] God's rejection of the poet is registered in terms of nature at its most aggressive. No shelter, no 'heaven-haven' seems available.

9] Hopkins questions the meaning and purpose of his suffering.

11–12] The joy and elation of Hopkins' acceptance of Christ are seen as short-lived compared with the agony of spirit experienced since he 'kissed the rod' of his vows.

14] (*my God!*): 'must be spoken in a horrified whisper' (W. H. Gardner).

No worst, there is none...

This sonnet (possibly dating from 1885) is written from the depths of that desolation of spirit described by St Ignatius: 'A darkening of the soul, trouble of mind, movement to base and earthly things, restlessness of various agitations and temptations, moving to distrust, loss of hope, loss of love; when the soul feels herself thoroughly apathetic, sad, and as it were separated from her Creator and Lord.'

1] The inversion of the word order, the double negative 'no... none', stress this outcry of despair.

Pitched past pitch of grief: the sense of being hurled like a helpless victim beyond the endurable limits of distress is overwhelmingly strong. Alliteration is never merely a poetic device in Hopkins' poetry. It has a dramatic meaningfulness. 'Pitch' also means defiled, and 'tuned too high'.

2] *schooled at forepangs:* taught by pangs suffered earlier, which looked forward to these.

wilder wring: the soul is twisted by an agony of distress.

3] *Comforter:* the Paraclete, Holy Ghost.

where, where: cf. 'The Wreck of the Deutschland', v. 3.

5] *My cries heave, herds-long:* my cries of agony lift up and follow one another, like cattle in a herd. 'Herds-long' also carries with it the sense of 'headlong', i.e. heave headlong... thus maintaining this sense of being lifted and thrown a great distance head foremost.

9] The distress and pain of spirit is enacted as a physical experience: a traveller in the mountains, perilously holding on to the scanty toeholds while beneath him abyss succeeds abyss.

11–12] *Nor does long our small | Durance deal:* the human capacity to endure this kind of peril is so slender.

The quiet close of the sonnet contrasts with the anguished opening. This is not 'the peace which passeth all understanding' but the exhaustion of body and soul alike accepting nervelessly the only respite (sleep) or refuge (death) that is available in these conditions.

I wake and feel the fell of dark...

Sleeplessness and darkness exacerbate Hopkins' mood of self-loathing and bitterness; and the unendurable agony that Christ is completely withdrawn from him.

1] *fell:* the hide or pelt of an animal. The visual sense aroused in 'dark' combines with the tactile to produce a feeling of suffocation (cf. *Macbeth*: 'the blanket of the dark'). 'Fell' also means 'strike down, kill', and 'dangerous'.

2] *hoürs:* the disyllable protracts the time suggested.

6] The time of agony is amplified by the stresses falling relentlessly on 'hours...years...life'.

7] *dead letters:* letters that cannot be delivered.

9-11] The physical sensation of the unhappy spiritual and mental state is felt most deeply by the opening metaphor/personifications 'gall...heartburn' which rise to the tortuous 'Selfyeast of spirit a dull dough sours'. The unleavened spirit is flat and rancid with despair.

13] *the lost:* those damned in Hell.

Thou art indeed just, Lord...

The epigraph is a quotation from Jer. xii. 1. 'Lord I know well that right is on thy side, if I plead against thee, yet remonstrate with thee I must; why is it that the affairs of the wicked prosper...? (Knox)

In a letter to Bridges (24 March 1889) Hopkins says 'Observe, it must be read *adagio molto* and with great stress.' The immense dignity of this sonnet, in which the sentence pattern is less elaborate and distorted than is usual in Hopkins, in no way diminishes its disturbing revelation of a life dedicated to God yet (apparently) impotent of worthy achievement.

8] *spare:* idle.

11] *fretty chervil:* the serrated, lace-like leaves of cow parsley.
Hopkins' overwhelming sense of the flourishing of the ways of sinners, 'the slots and thralls of lust'; and the world of nature, intensifies his anguish at his own creative barrenness.

13] *Time's eunuch:* Hopkins wrote to Bridges on 1 September 1885, 'if I could but get on, if I could but produce work, I should not mind its being buried, silenced, and going no further; but it kills me to be time's eunuch and never to beget' and—'Nothing comes: I am a eunuch—but it is for the kingdom of God's sake.'

THOMAS HARDY

Neutral Tones

Hardy was a poet even before he turned to writing novels. This poem, written in 1867 when he was twenty-seven, shows perfectly the cast of his mind. The human situation is matched by the environment. The chilling disenchantment with love and its deceptions is the human counterpart of the white sun and grayish leaves from, significantly, the ash tree. Though the setting matches the human experience, there is no sense that it is so because it is in sympathy with the human plight. The synchronization is fortuitous, and enhances the impression of tight-lipped bitterness principally given by the level tone and rhythm, varying only in the fourth line of each stanza, and rising a little to a controlled climax in the last stanza.

3] *starving:* cold, frozen (colloquial use), dying.
  sod: earth.

At Castle Boterel

'Castle Boterel' is in Cornwall. Hardy meditates on what he realizes is his last visit to the place where he met his first wife.

Time recollected is a recurring theme of Hardy's finest verse. Connected with this is an abiding sense of human transitoriness and the impermanence of human relationships existing in a setting that remains. Yet this is expressed as a vision of what happened once happening again: the old emotion is so strong that it is imagined as peopling the scene with ghosts, giving the landscape its intensest 'meaning' in its whole history. The earth only abides.

Readers of Hardy's novels will see affinities with Egdon Heath. D. H. Lawrence in his 'Study of Thomas Hardy' writes:

'The Heath persists. Its body is strong and fecund, it will bear many more crops beside this. Here is the sombre, latent power that will go on producing, no matter what happens to the product. Here is the deep, black source from whence all these little contents of lives are drawn. And the contents of the small lives are spilled and wasted.'

The poem opens and closes significantly in the drizzle which saddens the perspective on the dry and perfect moment, the indelible 'time of such quality'.

33] *my sand is sinking:* my time is running out (like sand in an hourglass).

Near Lanivet, 1872

Whereas 'At Castle Boterel' celebrates a recollected moment of perfection, this poem offers a painful, even harrowing experience which is registered as clearly in the deliberate awkwardness and hesitancy of the rhythm as in the subject matter itself. The intensity of the central stanzas of 'At Castle Boterel' has no place here: the uphill journey, symbolical of the journey through life, offers at its crest a momentary Golgotha in Cornwall. Characteristically the experience exists for a minute only. But this is long enough for it to etch its impression on the spirit so that it troubles like an uncanny premonition. The stunted handpost and the crossways take upon themselves in retrospect a haunting suggestiveness.

30] *the running of Time's far glass:* the hourglass image again.

After a Journey (Pentargan Bay)

Pentargan Bay is another of the scenes of Hardy's courtship in Cornwall. This poem explores an experience similar to that of 'The Voice'. Note the exactitude of Hardy's writing, arising from an overmastering awareness of a certain point in time, a particular place. An experience which in less sure hands could become vague and blurred is traced with uncompromising clarity of definition. Always the language and the way it moves are utilized in a stanza form which is fully expressive of the experience.

There is a superb analysis of this poem by F. R. Leavis in *Scrutiny*, vol. XIX, no. 2 (Winter 1952/3) which should be consulted.

The Voice

What strikes a reader in this exceptionally moving poem (written in 1912) is the expressive quality of the rhythm. The poem begins in a swinging ballad fashion; but this soon gives place to an unhappy listlessness of movement, eloquent of the poet's realization of his loss and desolation. The wind's sound becomes confused with the remembered once-loved voice and induces that faltering of mind and body which brings about the breakdown of the verse formation in the last stanza.

In the original text Hardy wrote 'existlessness' (line 11) and later replaced it with 'wan wistlessness'. Dr Leavis' comment is apt:

'"Existlessness"...is a questionable word, a characteristic eccentricity of invention; and yet here it sounds right. The touch that there may still be about the poem of what would normally have been rustic stiffness serves as a kind of guarantee of integrity.'

The Self-unseeing

An epitome of Hardy's elegiac art not only in its theme but in its subtlety of rhythm and economy of means.

The sense of the past pervading the present is communicated in the repeated 'Here' in the first stanza and is intensified by the shift back in tense from 'is' to 'was'. Place and time stimulate the poet's memory to recall his parents: the mother warm, comfortable, contented; the father ardent, playing his violin to her with fervour and devotion. The buoyancy of spirit reflected in the swift ecstatic rhythm rises in the first three lines of the third stanza ('danced', 'emblazoned', 'glowed') until with devastating shock, the dream collapses. In this trance of happiness, they looked outward, unaware of that happiness. Only now does Hardy see it as such, and of course it is lost.

The deft deployment of the pronoun sequence (they/she/he/I/we—time narrowing down to the painful point of the present) accounts for the succinctness and taut narrative line of the poem and enhances its final bitterness.

To an Unborn Pauper Child

The rhythm is halting, as if held back by misgiving about the whole nature of human destiny. Combined with this is the awkwardness of syntax and the clumsy use of unfamiliar words forced into strong rhythms ('The Doomsters heap / Travails and teens around us here') inherited in part from Browning. But the total impact of the poem lies in the combination of these unpromising constituents with a sincere and grave concern for the human lot. One of Hardy's principal qualities as a poet is his compassion.

4] *Doomsters:* the Fates. Curiously, Hardy often invoked them, while at the same time suggesting that he believed in no Providence, not even a malignant one.

5] *teens:* troubles.
26] *wold:* tract of land.

Midnight on the Great Western

The journey by train takes on wider implications particularly in the third and last verses where, with the buttressing power arising from the particularity of the opening two stanzas, Hardy is able to be more explicit about his theme. The moment of the boy seen with his twinkling key, his box and the ticket stuck in his hatband acts as a pinpoint of sharpest contrast to the vast regions of time and space that encompass him.

The passage might well be compared with the description of Father Time from *Jude the Obscure*. Whether the prose passage preceded the poem or vice versa it is hard to say. But the working over it twice at least argues its importance in Hardy's imagination.

4] *Bewrapt:* the coinage combines two senses: (1) wrapped up in a coat or rug, and falling asleep in the warmth; (2) 'rapt', in a trance-like state of visionary unknowingness.

Childhood among the Ferns

In her biography of her husband, F. E. Hardy writes:
'By the time he was fifteen, he tells us, he remembered lying back in the sun and wishing he need not grow up. He wanted to stay just as he was in the same place with the same few friends. The infinite possibilities that mature life held for failure and suffering appalled him, made him sink back into such security as he knew.'

The poem creates the situation of this impulse to withdraw from life, centring it on an experience of childhood. Especially notable is the way in which Hardy vividly communicates the tenuous security against the storms of life offered by the house of ferns. Even in this poem of withdrawal, Hardy's characteristic honesty makes itself felt:

'Making pretence I was not rained upon.'

7] *spray-roofed house:* house made of the sprays of fern, and sprayed by the rain.

During Wind and Rain

The folk-song influence is marked in the patterning of events in a seasonal cycle and in the refrains with slight but meaningful variations which gather about themselves regrets and ironies as the poem moves forward. The sensation of Time overcoming happy human companionship and endeavour is brought home by the affectionate exactitude of trivial domestic details set over against the images in the last line of each stanza. (See Douglas Brown, *ThomasHardy* (Longmans Green, 1961), pp. 147–52.)

28] *carved:* on tombstones.

Friends Beyond

This is Hardy's 'Elegy in a Country Churchyard'. A comparison with Gray's poem might prove rewarding; it would illuminate, by contrast, the nature of Hardy's ideas and expression.

Hardy feels instinctively drawn to the notion of human transience as well as to human achievement. He creates compassionately a sense of past generations who have found some fulfilment in their rural callings or in rural society and traditions. But he is also aware that the problems and distractions of the human condition find their real solution only in death with its ironically effortless achievement of indifference.

If, however, the poem offered only this moralizing it would not be particularly distinguished. What makes it memorable is the rich particularity of occupations and possessions; the sensuous exactness of time and place; the curious words ('stillicide', 'fellow-wight') which have an unusual effectiveness; and the sensitive shift of the rhythm animating just sufficiently the long line and the wavering verse formation.

7] *fellow-wight:* fellow mortal.
9] *stillicide:* the noise of dripping water in a cave that vexes the silence.
10] *the bane:* the poison (death).
16] *mid:* may.
21] *con:* read over.
22] *let the charlock grow:* charlock is a weed that grows in corn.
23] *Foul the grinterns:* a grintern is a compartment in a granary (*N.E.D.*).
24] *ho:* bother.
30] *stage:* the stage coach bringing the mails.
31] *freed those crosses:* freed from those troubles and anxieties.
32] *the Trine:* the Three Fates; or perhaps the Christian Trinity.

Drummer Hodge

This poem, concerned with the fate of a young English countryman in the Boer War, is as strongly patterned and direct in language as a ballad. In each verse the first two lines are concerned with Hodge; first as he is now, next what he was before enlistment and finally what he will be. The next two pairs of lines in each verse concern the 'foreignness' of the land in which he has fought and died and the equally alien nature of the constellations wheeling above him. The unfamiliarity of both sky and earth serves to underline Hardy's sense of a universe apathetic to the tragic lot of man. By a sharp twist of circumstance, the homely local farmhand becomes a part of this alien landscape. The macabre ballad image of the tree (this time deliberately vague because unnamed) with its roots feeding on the young man's corpse brings home this idea with great power.

Title] *Hodge:* the traditional name for an English country labourer.
3] *kopje:* Afrikaans name for a small hill.
4] *veldt:* Afrikaans for a tract of bush country.
5] *west:* move westwards through the sky.
9] *Karoo:* elevated plateau of clayey soil in South Africa, waterless in the dry season.

W.B.YEATS

The Fascination of What's Difficult

F. R. Leavis comments on this poem and others from *The Green Helmet* (1912):

'It is hard to believe that the characteristic verse of the later volume [i.e. *The Green Helmet*] comes from the same hand as that of the earlier. The new verse has no incantation, no dreary, hypnotic rhythm: it belongs to the actual, waking world, and is in the idiom and movement of modern speech. It is spare, hard and sinewy and in tone sardonic, expressing the bitterness and disillusion of a man who has struggled and been frustrated...To pass from the earlier verse to this is something like passing from Campion to Donne. The parallel, indeed, is not so random as it might seem. At any rate, Donne's name in connection with a poet capable of passionate intellectual interests, who from such a start achieved such a manner, leads us to reflect that if the poetic tradition of the nineteenth century had been less completely unlike the Metaphysical tradition, Mr Yeats might have spent less of his power outside his poetry.'

4] *our colt:* Pegasus, the winged horse, symbol of poetry. The winged horse imagery is brilliantly worked out, particularly in lines 6, 7 and 8. Yeats uses the Pegasus symbol memorably in 'Easter 1916' and 'Coole and Ballylee'.

The Wild Swans at Coole

Coole House was the home of Lady Gregory. Yeats was a frequent visitor.

'Coole House, though it has lost the great park full of ancient trees, is still set in the midst of a thick wood, which spreads out behind the house in two directions, in one along the edges of a lake which, as there is no other escape for the water except a narrow subterranean passage, doubles or trebles its size in winter. In later years I was to know the edges of that lake better than any spot on earth, to know it in all the changes of the seasons, to find out there always some new beauty.'

Yeats, *Autobiographies*, 'Dramatis Personae', pp. 388–9

2–3] As in 'Coole Park and Ballylee' the season accords with Yeats' own age. He had reached middle years, the autumn of his life. His sensation of the onset of old age is sharpened by the contrast with the apparent agelessness and perennial beauty of the swans.

11–12] The presentation of the rising swans is superbly concrete. Is the reader meant to envisage the birds tracing out a gyre-like pattern in the sky?

13–18] The resonant vitality of the swans' flight throws into relief Yeats' own disenchantment; his disappointments in love, the bitter sense of frustration engendered by his advancing years.

19–24] The swans, moving with the same ease and majesty in the lake as in the air, become symbols of eternity, triumphing over time in absolute fidelity to each other. 'Companionable' (line 21) takes the full stress of the line: it serves to make the following lines the more disquieting.

In Memory of Major Robert Gregory

Major Robert Gregory was Lady Gregory's only son. An airman, he was killed on 23 January 1918 in action. Apart from his other accomplishments, Robert Gregory had considerable skill as a painter and designed sets for some of the plays at the Abbey Theatre. This poem should be read in conjunction with 'An Irish Airman Foresees his Death'.

1] *our house:* The tower at Thoor Ballylee. For the first time this tower takes its place in Yeats' poetry. Yeats had bought it (for £35) in 1917 and he was hoping to restore it with Robert Gregory's help.

Note the easy, conversational tone and diction of the opening verses, the colloquial freedom of the rhythm subtly and significantly changing in the last line of the first verse. The second verse is built on a similar pattern.

9] *we'd have the new friend meet the old:* Yeats refers to himself and his wife. Unterecker says that the first two stanzas are 'a conversation with the new bride about the complexities of friendship for the sake of which even the most happily married couples quarrel'.

The poem now opens out fully to the three friends Lionel Johnson, J. M. Synge and George Pollexfen, all of whom represent individually a partial excellence. The qualities in each of these men are blended in Robert Gregory's character and achievements.

17] *Lionel Johnson:* 1867–1902, poet (a member of the Rhymers' Club, one of the companions of the Cheshire Cheese), Catholic convert, and scholar.

19] *Though courteous:* Yeats values this aristocratic quality in Johnson.

much falling: see Johnson's poem 'Mystic and Cavalier' quoted by Yeats in the *Autobiographies:* 'Go from me: I am one of those who fall.'

25] *that enquiring man, John Synge:* John Millington Synge (1871–1909), poet and playwright of the plays of Abbey Theatre's finest period, e.g. *Riders to the Sea, The Well of the Saints, The Playboy of the Western World,* etc. He died at the early age of thirty-eight. Yeats recounts in detail his meeting with Synge in Paris and how he persuaded him to seek his inspiration in the Aran Islands, in *Essays* pp. 298, 299. This explains the second, fifth and seventh lines of the stanza. Of Synge in the wild Blaskets and Inishmaan, Yeats writes: 'Here were men and women who under the weight of their necessity lived, as the artists live, in the presence of death and childhood, and the great affections and orgiastic moment when life outleaps its limits, and who, as it is always with those who have refused or escaped the trivial and the temporary, had dignity and good manners where manners mattered.'

30] *a most desolate stony place:* the Aran Islands. In *Autobiographies* Yeats writes: 'I had just come from Aran, and my imagination was full of those grey islands where men must reap with knives because of the stones.'

33] *old George Pollexfen:* Yeats' uncle, who lived in Sligo. See the biographical introduction.

39] *By opposition, square and trine:* George Pollexfen's astrological calculations.

41-8] Yeats, having evoked memories of his three friends, accommodates himself to their deaths. But now the poem moves towards a climax as Robert Gregory's recent death is contemplated, a loss both personal and national. The diction never loses its sobriety nor the rhythm its dignity.

46] *my dear friend:* Lady Gregory.

47] *Our Sidney:* Sir Philip Sidney: the flower of sixteenth-century courtesy; courtier, soldier, poet and horseman. Sidney fulfils, in his versatility, the ideal of Renaissance manhood.

48] *that discourtesy of death:* Death is looked upon as a discourtesy, an act of crude hostility directed against the passionately civilized. Compare the remark about Johnson.

57–64] A brilliant evocation of horseriding prowess. The stanza gains power by its contrast with verse 7 which celebrates in its particularity the landscape at Thoor Ballylee. The enjambments at ends of lines 60 and 61 enact the leap and the astonished meet's misgiving.

64] The physical prowess is ironically superseded.

67] *that stern colour and that delicate line:* even the painterly concerns are seen in terms of moral or knightly ideal.

81] *Some burn damp faggots:* those whose life slowly smoulders away without the heat and light of passionate vision or energy.

82–4] In contrast are those, like Gregory, whose lives are burnt out swiftly in a single intense flare of dazzling radiance. The consequent blackness is the more bewildering.

The last stanza recapitulates the theme of the three men of the earlier part of the poem: 'manhood tried'—Synge; 'childhood loved'—George Pollexfen; 'boyish intellect approved'—Lionel Johnson.

96] Louis Unterecker writes:

'This last line, ironical and grand in its announcement that Yeats' own eloquence must lift into silence before a theme larger than eloquence itself, lets the poem end where it had begun: in the stillness that surrounds an imaginary statement before an imagined fire...'

An Irish Airman Foresees his Death

Major Gregory is seen as meditating on his particular rôle as airman in the 1914–18 war; caring less for the outcome of the conflict than for the impulse that brought him into it; and the insight granted upon the acting on that impulse. The laconic acceptance of his 'fate', his clear-eyed, even curt resignation to the part he finds himself playing, is attended by a mature balance, an equipoise of mood and character. He is, at the same time, wholly committed, yet aloof.

Throughout the poem, Yeats balances opposing ideas (fight/guard, years to come/years behind) and phrases, thus making the words and syntax enact the experience explored.

3–4] Though the Irish had cause to hate the English, Major Gregory was fighting on the English side against Germany. (Lady Gregory had strongly favoured Irish participation in the war. Yeats, too accepted the view that Irish Nationalists should co-operate with England.)

Easter 1916

This poem was written shortly after the Easter Rising, although not published for general circulation until 1921. The Easter Rising was an outbreak of armed revolt in Dublin by Irish Nationalists against the British authorities.

It was suppressed after some bloodshed and the leaders (named at the end of the poem) were executed by the British. In a letter to Lady Gregory, after the Easter Rising had taken place and the harsh sentences had been passed on the participants, Yeats writes:

'I have little doubt there have been many miscarriages of justice...I am trying to write a poem on the men executed—"terrible beauty has been born again"...I had no idea that any public event could so deeply move me—and I am very despondent about the future.' Of Maud Gonne's response to the tragedy (her husband, Sean Macbride, was one of the leaders executed) he continues: 'Her main thought seems to be "tragic dignity has returned to Ireland".'

The poem celebrates the men who were executed for the part they played in the Easter Rising and also defines Yeats' changed attitude to them and the tragic event.

1–16] Yeats states his 'relationship' with the rebels: they, deeply and passionately committed to the course of action, wholly devoted to Irish Nationalism, even (as events proved) to the point of death; Yeats sympathetic, yet detached, insulated by irony.

2] *vivid faces:* the ardour of the rebels gives a keenness to the glance.

3] *from counter or desk:* the ordinariness, the humdrum commonplaceness of the rebels' daily life and work are stressed. These are not the nobility, yet they will achieve heroic stature.

3–4] *grey | Eighteenth century houses:* It is likely that Yeats wishes to convey a sense of drab dignity, restraint, even civic decorum, by this heavily stressed line.

5 et seq.] Yeats emphasises his detachment with the repetition of 'polite meaningless words', convinced that both the rebels and he are merely acting a part ('where motley is worn'); both he and they, he implies, are fools, victims of their own dreams, heroic or otherwise.

The off-hand tone suddenly changes to the shocked urgency and bewilderment of the last two lines of the stanza. The unexpected event, in these circumstances, with these protagonists, works its disturbing spiritual and moral metamorphosis.

17–40] Yeats catalogues some of the men (and a woman) concerned most closely with the Easter Rising, detailing here the 'change' from their rôles in the 'casual comedy' of day-to-day living, to the terrible and violent figures they become under the impact of the event.

17] *That woman:* Constance Markiewicz (née Gore-Booth) had carried arms in the Easter Rising. The troop she led was one of the last to surrender. She was not shot but imprisoned. (See 'In memory of Eva Gore-Booth and Con Markiewicz'). The poignant memory of her as a young woman, beautiful, riding to harriers, is sharpened when Yeats sees what she has now become, her loveliness betrayed by participation in political rant.

24] *This man:* Padraic Pearse (1879–1916). He had founded St Enda's School. He was also president of the provisional government in Easter Week and surrendered in the Post Office.

25] *rode our winged horse:* Pearse had written and published prose and poetry in Gaelic and English. The 'winged horse', as usual in Yeats, the Irish literary movement.

26] *his helper and friend:* Thomas MacDonagh (1878–1916), writer of poetry and criticism. He was the author of *Literature in Ireland*.

'Met MacDonagh yesterday—a man with some literary faculty which will probably come to nothing through lack of culture and encouragement...in England this man would have been remarkable in some way; here he is being crushed by the mechanical logic and commonplace eloquence which give power to the most empty mind.'

Yeats, *Autobiographies*, 'Estrangement', p. 488.

32] *A drunken, vainglorious lout:* Major Sean Macbride, who had married Maud Gonne in 1903. The marriage was dissolved later. The 'bitter wrong' had been done to Maud Gonne. Yeats puts Macbride at the climax of his list, a gesture of magnanimity and admiration. Whatever Macbride was has been transcended by his daring and valour during the Easter Rising and his consequent political martyrdom. The braggadocio 'actor' has become hero. Note Yeats' self-accusatory 'I had dreamed'.

41–56] And yet, compared with the life of flux about them, these men and this woman have not changed. The devotion to the cause has petrified the heart so that it only troubles the living stream with its stony presence. Their passionate devotion is a kind of enchantment which precludes the spontaneity of life brilliantly suggested by the intricacy of syntax, the flow and pause of rhythm in the second sentence of this stanza.

43] *Enchanted to a stone:* the phrase carries the suggestion of those folk-tales in which people are turned into stones. The hardness and callousness of the revolutionary is also evoked. Yeats implicitly criticizes this.

57–80] The stony 'enchantment' has been paid for at the price of the rebels' lives. Yeats now affirms their tragic self-sacrifice so that the dead men attain the dignity of the Irish legendary heroes.

65–6] Yeats takes refuge momentarily in the image of nightfall—but rejects it in the next line by stating the bleak inescapable fact.

68–9] The long, unhappy problem of Anglo-Irish relations is succinctly, pessimistically evoked.

78] *Wherever green is worn:* the Irish national colour. Cf. the patriotic song 'The Wearing of the Green'.

On a Political Prisoner

The 'Political Prisoner' of the poem (written in 1918) was the Countess Markievicz (Constance Gore-Booth). She had been implicated in the Easter Rising and was imprisoned in Holloway Gaol. The poem 'In memory of Eva Gore-Booth and Constance Markiewicz', written much later, should also be consulted. These poems are eloquent of Yeats' hatred of political fanaticism.

1–2] The imposed patience, nourished by hatred, of the prison cell, contrasts bitterly and ironically with her youthful lack of it.

7–12] The freedom and poised beauty of the bird becomes a symbol of the Countess before she dedicated her life to political schemes.

11] *Blind and leader of the blind:* a reference to the proverb, 'If the blind lead the blind both shall fall into the ditch', Matt. xv. 14. Those who have no perception of what their thoughts and actions will lead to. Jeffares suggests that 'the blind' may refer to her bohemian life in Dublin.

There is a famous picture by Breughel illustrating this theme of the blind leading the blind. Yeats may well have had this in mind.

12] The implications of the 'foul ditch' are in strongest contrast to the associations of the 'hollows of the sea'.

lie: John Unterecker indicates a pun on this word.

17-24] Diction, rhythm and syntax work together to communicate the sense of the sea-bird in its hovering movement *above* 'the hollows of the sea'.

The Second Coming

1] *the widening gyre:* the 'gyre' recurs so frequently in Yeats' later poetry that it is essential to understand what Yeats wishes to convey. Here is his explanation from *A Vision*:

'A line is a symbol of time, and expresses a movement, symbolising the emotional subjective mind, without extension in space; a plane cutting the line at right angles is spatial, the symbol of objectivity and intellect. A gyre is a combination of line and plane, and as one tendency or the other must always be stronger, the gyre is always expanding or contracting. The gyre is drawn as a cone which represents sometimes the individual soul and its history, sometimes general life. For this two cones are substituted, since neither the soul of man or nature can be expressed without conflict.'

The word is associated with the spiralling flight of a falcon (symbol here of the aspiring human mind) and the failure of the falconer, Christ, or whoever should be the master of the falcon to reach or control the bird which is now swinging outwards and upwards to its destruction. It is important to understand what Yeats means by a gyre because, once grasped, the image has a remarkable power to arrest the attention and focus the imagination in a symbol which is amplified and illuminated by the succeeding lines of the poem. See also T. R. Henn, *The Lonely Tower*, pp. 185-7. Mr Henn has an excellent diagram of a gyre on p. 187.

3-8] Yeats foresees the coming era of violence and destruction. The poetry has a disturbing vatic force which arises partly from the physical turbulence of the verbs; and partly from the images of irresistible flood waters.

9-11] The disintegration of order and tradition based on Christian values presages a forthcoming event of great terror as devastating as the Second Coming of Christ (cf. the visions of the Book of Revelation).

12] *a vast image:* it is difficult to explain precisely Yeats' 'vast image'. T. R. Henn suggests a number of sources for this particular image—the Egyptian sphinx; late nineteenth-century drawings; Blake's illustration of Beatrice addressing Dante from her chariot drawn by mythical beasts; and the Lion of St Mark in Venice. It may be one of these or all of them. What emerges from the lines is that the shape is endowed with a sinister power, bestial and fantastic, a source of destruction and doom. Mr Henn continues: 'The general meaning is perhaps that the premonition of a new era causes this stirring of the eternal and inexorable power in history that is latent in the desert from which prophets and revolutions come; Christianity has brought strife and discord. Now the period of two thousand years is closing. The next era will follow the same pattern; but in *opposition* to it.'

The image is considerably sharpened by its association with the customary ideas that spring from the 'rocking cradle' (line 20) and 'Bethlehem'. Note the implications of 'slouches' (line 22).

'*Spiritus Mundi*': a kind of corporate imagination. The 'rough beast' and the 'vast image' arise from the poet's storehouse of images and are embodied by him in the poem.

A Prayer for my Daughter

Anne Butler Yeats was born on 24 February 1919. 'I think a daughter (family ambition and disappointed relatives apart) pleases me...' The poem was begun a few weeks after her birth and completed in June at Ballylee. It should be read with 'The Second Coming' in mind.

2] Anne Yeats had a seventeenth-century cradle, hence the reference to 'cradle-hood and coverlid'.

It is characteristic of Yeats' poetry of this period that this poem begins so firmly in a particular place at a particular time. From this point, immediate and specific, the poet moves effortlessly on into a more searching exploration and development of his theme.

4] *Gregory's wood*: one of the woods on Coole demesne, Lady Gregory's estate in Galway.

5] The haystack suggests necessary food; the roof the home, the shelter. Both are man-made constructions. Both are vulnerable to destruction in a time of war.

The storm Yeats presents so vividly at the outset of this poem (see the second stanza) gathers a disturbing quality. Note the verbs, the repeated 'scream'. It becomes the 'storm' that will wreck what Yeats prizes most of European civilization.

10] *scream upon the tower*: again, the specific 'tower': Yeats' Tower (Thoor Ballylee) and also 'an image of mysterious wisdom won by toil'.

13–16] cf. 'The Second Coming', lines 1–8.

17–24] Yeats values women's beauty: but he values their sympathy, intuition and compassion far more.

25] *Helen*: the daughter of Leda and the Swan. She was the wife of Menelaus but was abducted by Paris and carried to Troy.

26] *a fool*: Paris, son of Priam, King of Troy.

27] *that great Queen*: Venus, Goddess of Love. See Botticelli's painting, *The Birth of Venus*.

29] *a bandy-leggèd smith*: Vulcan, armourer of the Gods.

30–2] It is likely that Yeats is drawing on his own experience here, and the sudden marriage of Maud Gonne with Sean Macbride is being hinted at. The waywardness of a woman's choice of a lover fascinates and bewilders Yeats.

32] *Horn of Plenty*: in addition to its strong sexual implications the phrase suggests liberality, magnanimity—probably akin to what Chaucer meant by the word '*fredom*'. The phrase also implies that a beautiful woman's perverse predilection for an inappropriate mate diminishes a full realization of the potential richness of their union.

33] *courtesy*: Yeats implies more than good manners. The verbs at the end of lines 33 and 34 which take the stress of the voice imply a moral effort of the finest delicacy that courtesy necessitates if it is to be something more than a surface quality.

41–8] The 'flourishing hidden tree' and the 'green laurel' share with the chestnut tree in 'Among School Children' a suggestion of the quality of blessedness. Note how the verb 'rooted' takes the full weight at the outset of line 48. The need to find a 'dear perpetual place' to be rooted in seems essential if one is to withstand the storms, both personal and universal, of the twentieth century.

49–56] Thoughts of the Countess Markiewicz and Maud Gonne are clearly in Yeats' mind. It is essential to read (1) lines 17–23 'Easter 1916'; (2) 'On a Political Prisoner'; (3) 'In Memory of Eva Gore-Booth and Con Markiewicz'.

57–64] Note Yeats' characteristic dislike of 'opinions'. The worst kind of hatred is the hatred based upon abstract thought.

73–4] *a house | Where all's accustomed, ceremonious:* Yeats stresses the value of inherited traditions, habits of thought and behaviour which have been passed down through generations and, in the process, have been dignified and refined by time and human endeavour. He may have in his mind the 'courtesy' as well as 'the inherited glory of the rich' which he encountered at Lady Gregory's house at Coole.

75–6] *arrogance and hatred are the wares | Peddled in the thoroughfares:* Yeats may be lashing out at bourgeois values in the implication of 'wares peddled in the thoroughfares'. Thoughts of the part played by Maud Gonne in stirring up political agitation may also be implicit in these lines. See 'No Second Troy', lines 1–4.

Sailing to Byzantium

The significance of Byzantium is important to Yeats at this period of his life and poetry. It represents a multiple symbolic value. In *A Vision* Yeats writes:

'I think that in early Byzantium, maybe never before or since in recorded history, religious, aesthetic and practical life were one, that architect and artificers...spoke to the multitude and the few alike. The painter, the mosaic worker, the worker in gold and silver, the illuminator of sacred books, were almost impersonal, almost perhaps without consciousness of individual design, absorbed in the subject matter and that the vision of a whole people.'

It represents for him a perfected symbol of the much-sought unity that he had striven for all his creative life. It also embodies the permanence of Art set in sharpest contrast with the transitoriness of human life.

1] *That is no country for old men:* Yeats has reached old age. He realizes he has no place in the land he has grown up in, Ireland. He seeks now the serenity, order and beauty not to be found in the country of his youth and early manhood with its ardour, sensual passion and division against itself.

1–8] The images of *natural* life, the young in love, are emphasized by the fish images, suggestive of teeming life, and flashing, lithe movement. The zest and vitality intensify by contrast Yeats' old age. The images of what is *natural* are dramatically contrasted with the permanence of art: the 'birds in the trees' and the golden bird in the last stanza of the poem.

8] *Monuments of unageing intellect:* the art of Byzantium.

11] *Soul clap its hands and sing:* the source of this may be Blake's statement that, at his brother Robert's death, he saw his brother's soul leaving the dead body and ascend heavenward clapping its hands for joy.

13] *singing school:* there is no 'school': the poet must school himself by a study of the great imaginative and artistic achievements of the past.

14] *Monuments of its own magnificence:* verse or any artistic creation.

16] *the holy city of Byzantium:* not only is Byzantium 'holy' because of its importance as a great religious centre, but because it is a place where the creative spirit is working at its best.

17–18] *O sages standing in God's holy fire | As in the gold mosaic of a wall:* images in mosaic against their glittering background of gold (cf. the Ravenna Mosaics which Yeats had first seen in 1907) as well as the saints who are caught up in the fire of Heaven and are thus transfigured. God is the supreme artificer, like the poet a 'maker'—but the Maker of All Things.

19] *Perne in a gyre:* to perne is to move with a circular spinning motion—the perne was another name for a spool on which the thread is wound.

19–20] 'The juxtaposition of fire and music may be traced back to his statement in "Per Amica Silentia Lunae" that "In the condition of fire is all music and rest"' (Richard Ellmann).

21] *Consume my heart away:* the heart is a source of pain. Old men have only their minds. Hence the valuation set upon the 'monuments of unageing intellect'.

24] *the artifice of eternity:* God is seen as the great craftsman creating the perfection of Eternity as the artist strives to attain perfection in his art.

25–6] The natural life, so magnificently celebrated in the opening stanza, is rejected in favour of the 'golden bird', the artefact, whose song to the transient generations is 'of what is past and passing and to come'.

29] *a drowsy Emperor:* Yeats may also have had in his mind the Hans Andersen fairy story of 'The Nightingale'.

30] *Or set upon a golden bough to sing:* the golden bird symbolizes a reconciliation of opposites—the transient and the temporal with the permanent. Yeats would have liked his bird to have the qualities of eternity, but as it is an artefact, though of the purest and most durable of metals, it is subject to the metamorphosis of Time.

Leda and the Swan

This sonnet enacts the union of Leda and Zeus who appeared to her in the form of a swan. From their union Helen was born—and, by implication, the siege and destruction of Troy and the murder of Agamemnon, the Greek commander.

The sonnet was suggested by Michelangelo's painting, a coloured reproduction of which was in Yeats' possession. In *A Vision* he writes:

'I imagine the annunciation that founded Greece as made to Leda remembering that they showed in a Spartan temple, strung up to the roof as a holy relic, an unhatched egg of hers; and that from one of her eggs came Love and from the other War.'

Among School Children

The poem was written on 26 September 1926.

8] *A sixty-year-old smiling public man:* Yeats had been made a Senator of the Irish Free State in 1922, as a reward for his services to Ireland. In 1924 he had been awarded the Nobel Prize for Literature.

9] *a Ledaean body:* Leda was the mother of Helen, the father being Jove in the form of a swan. See 'Leda and the Swan'. The 'Ledaean body' is, in all likelihood, that of Maud Gonne.

10] *a sinking fire:* the phrase carries overtones of old age when the passions and energies of youth have burnt themselves to their last glowing embers.

15–16] An image of harmony and kinship derived from Plato's image in the *Symposium* of the twin halves of a sphere, the most perfect and inscrutable of forms, symbol of eternity.

17–24] Yeats is reminded of the girlhood of the woman he loved; and the thought gathers poignancy from what she is now (verse IV) contrasted with what she was then. The disenchantment that attends upon middle and old age is heightened by the contrast with childhood and youth.

20–1] The descendants of the swan (Zeus) and Leda are endowed with their mother's grace, distinction and beauty—at least in childhood.

26] *Quattrocento finger:* a synecdoche for a fifteenth-century Italian painter. Although he had Leonardo da Vinci in mind, Yeats avoids using the name of a particular painter and chooses to evoke a richness of association by the use of the term 'Quattrocento'—the century in which Italian painting reached a peak of achievement. (Yeats had a deep interest in painting. His father and his brother were both excellent painters—particularly his brother. Yeats himself had also had training as a painter. He had first-hand knowledge of Renaissance paintings in the National Gallery but it was on his visit to Italy with Lady Gregory in 1907 that he saw the vast collections of Italian painting which had such a profound effect on his mind and art.)

29–30] The poet is reminded of his own boyhood and early manhood when he was handsome enough; this painful thought is swiftly suppressed as this is no occasion for nostalgia for one's lost years. With the nun and the school-children present and himself acting 'in a public capacity' he must at least appear 'comfortable'.

30] *pretty plumage:* Jeffares says that this refers to Yeats' raven-coloured hair.

32] *scarecrow:* Yeats' tragi-comic image of old age—points forward to line 48. See also 'Sailing to Byzantium', lines 9–10. Yeats' disparaging reference to himself represents what he sees himself as *in essence*. In actual fact he was particularly distinguished in appearance, his natural dignity enhanced by a fine sartorial sense.

33] *a shape upon her lap:* the new born baby.

34] *Honey of generation:* a difficult phrase. Yeats' note on this stanza is not altogether helpful. 'I have taken the "honey of generation" from Porphyry's essay on "The Cave of the Nymphs", but find no warrant in it for considering it the "drug" that destroys the "recollection" of pre-natal freedom. He blamed a cup of oblivion given in the zodiacal sign of Cancer.'

The phrase could mean that it is the child who is, so to speak, 'betrayed' into birth, into life, by the mother; or the pleasure of generation betrays the mother into conceiving her child.

35] The verbs suggest the physical sensation of childbirth.

36] *recollection:* in neo-Platonic thought the soul after birth forgot the world it had come from.

the drug: a drink (perhaps associated with the 'honey' above) which makes the soul forget its 'pre-natal freedom'.

41–8] *Plato, Aristotle, Pythagoras:* Greek philosophers who each had theories about the relation of the body and the soul. The following comment on verse VI is is illuminating:

'The language is light-hearted but not shallow: there is a depth of admiration in the sketches of all these philosophers. There is also irony in the punning play upon "play" that carries him from Plato's belittling of phenomena to the practical Aristotle's buttock drumming, and thence to the Pythagorean music of the spheres. It prepares for their abrupt dismissal, and the sudden descent from the romantic phrasing of lines 5, 6, 7 to the racy idiom is a dramatic use of language whch delivers judgement by changing perspective.'   A. G. Stock, *W. B. Yeats, His Poetry and Thought*

42] *paradigm:* example, pattern, especially of inflexion of noun, verb (*S.O.E.D.*). Yeats is using the word, a grammatical term, metaphorically. (Cf. John Wain, *Interpretations* (Routledge and Kegan Paul, 1955): 'What precise associations the word paradigm had for Yeats I do not know; in my experience I have seldom met it except in the pages of a Greek grammar, where it meant the schema of the intellectual parts of a verb: an excellent parallel for the intellectually conceived framework which gives shape and body to the 'spume' that plays on it. These two lines alone would prove that Yeats was a great poet, if nothing else of his had survived.')

43] *taws:* leather thong.

44] *a king of kings:* Alexander the Great. Aristotle was his tutor.

47] *careless:* without anxiety.

48] *Old clothes upon old sticks:* the philosophers, for all their wisdom, add up to very little. They too, are in their way, scarecrows. Yeats is fascinated by and yet distrusts philosophy. It is significant in Yeats' play *The Hour Glass* that it is the Fool, not the worn-out Wise Man, who enjoys what triumph there is in that morality play.

49–51] Yeats draws a parallel between the love of the mother for son and the love of the nun for what the image of the Virgin or saint represents. The mother's 'image' is not her actual son, now grown to maturity; but an ideal of him, as he was as a boy, youth, distinguished poet. Both nun and mother suffer: the mother before her son's imagined suffering and growth, the nun as a consequence of the hard demands of the religious life. It is important to remember that the images, the objects of 'piety and affection', are un-ageing, they are 'self-born' and therefore symbols of 'heavenly glory'. By comparison with them, 'man's enterprise' (cf. the philosophers) is very near a mockery.

57–64] The final stanza explores and defines what Yeats means by 'heavenly glory', at first negatively and then affirmatively in the symbols of the chestnut tree and the dance. The first four lines of the stanza draw together the earlier themes of the poem: the last four apostrophize on a note of triumphant secular adoration 'the completed symbol of heavenly glory' (Ellmann).

57] *Labour:* the poem has presented the reader with labour in three aspects— the labour of the children at their school-work, the labour of the mother in childbirth and finally the philosophers' 'labouring after truth'. Playing across all these is the notion of the labour of various aspects of love.

John Wain's analysis of this poem in *Interpretations* is worth study. The relevant chapter on 'The Tree and The Dance' in Frank Kermode's *Romantic Image* (Routledge and Legan Paul, 1957) throws an interesting light on the last four lines.

In Memory of Eva Gore-Booth and Con Markiewicz

In the winter of 1894–5 Yeats visited Lissadell, the Georgian mansion near Sligo of Sir Henry Gore-Booth, where he met the daughters of this enlightened Protestant family. He was deeply impressed by the ordered graciousness of living and aristocratic vitality of the Gore-Booths. This elegy was written thirty-three years later when Yeats was staying at Seville in Spain. 'Easter 1916' and 'On a Political Prisoner' should be studied in conjunction with this poem.

1–4] The delicacy of the opening four lines, evoking by their specificity and word movement the unspoilt beauty of the two girls, haunts the rest of the poem. The girls become symbolic victims of the ravages of time and political commitment. The memory of their beauty however asserts itself with ironic pathos in the repetition of the opening in lines 16–20.

21] *Dear shadows:* the girls, now women who have become embroiled in the affairs of the world of politics and philanthrophy, are but ghosts of their former selves. The phrase links up with and modifies the earlier harshness of 'withered old and skeleton-gaunt' and harmonizes it with the opening lines of the poem.

23] *a common wrong or right:* i.e. not only 'communal' but also 'low'.

25] *Have no enemy but time:* the ravages of political action are less than those of time. Yeats sees the need to vanquish Time in the moment of illumination at the place of vision.

30] *we the great gazebo built:* a gazebo is a summerhouse built at a point of vantage in a fine landscape to give the best views. The gazebo is both fact and symbol, evoking simultaneously the great landscape gardens of the eighteenth century (and, by implication, Lissadell which is a Georgian house) and also the crystal house of culture, 'the nineteenth century's dream of an ordered civilisation' (Unterecker).

31] *They convicted us of guilt:* 'guilt' in the sense, perhaps, of responsibility for stirring up political feeling to a pitch of intensity. Cf. Yeats' lines:

> 'Did that play of mine send out
> Certain men the English shot?'

'They' most likely refers to the revolutionaries. There is a possibility that 'they' are the 'sages', the wise old men who would deplore this 'folly of fight / With a common wrong or right'.

Coole Park and Ballylee, 1931

The poem starts at Thoor Ballylee. (See Hone, *W. B. Yeats*, p. 319.)

4] *Raftery:* a blind Irish poet. (There is a chapter on Raftery in Yeats' *The Celtic Twilight*.)

6] *Coole demesne:* Lady Gregory's estate.

8] *What's water but the generated soul:* Yeats took this idea from Porphyry: 'In the Cave of the Nymphs': souls descending into generation fly to moisture.

The last line of this stanza carries the whole weight of the implications of the preceding lines, as well as establishing the harmonious link between himself and Lady Gregory. Yeats also sees the water as symbolizing the soul passing from the light 'undimmed in Heaven's face' (which is life), through darkness (the 'dark cellar') which is death, to reappear in the lake in Coole demesne—the soul reincarnated.

12] *For Nature's pulled her tragic buskin on:* Nature seen as Art: the world in winter dress, the season according with old age and death. Lady Gregory died in 1932 when Yeats was working on the poem, and he was in his mid-sixties. The winter trees, now 'dry sticks', may have some connotation with dying civilization of the twentieth century.

13] *rant:* the colloquial word gives a touch of 'common things' without strain or intrusion.

14] *At sudden thunder of the mounting swan:* cf. 'The Wild Swans at Coole'. The swan is seen as an emblem of the soul.

17] *That stormy white:* the swan.

In the next three lines Yeats uses the swan's journey as an emblem of the soul's progress. Note the vigour and beauty of the 'swan' and the assured ring of the rhythm that celebrates it.

25-32] The poem moves now to a magnificent retrospective assessment in poetic terms of Lady Gregory, Coole and the civilization that she and the noble house represent.

25-6] Lady Gregory is an invalid; she passes from room to room with great difficulty. Hear the repeated hollowness of 'sound...sound' broken up by 'stick'; the irksomeness of movement implied in 'toils'.

27 et seq.] But the movement is through a house which has stood for the finest aspects of country house civilization. Here is a permanent achievement even though the house stands on the brink of demolition and Lady Gregory is its 'last inheritor'. (Coole was demolished in the 1930s.) See also *Autobiographies*, pp. 388-95, for an excellent description of Coole House, its owners and its contents.

34] *once more dear than life:* Yeats was a frequent visitor to Coole House and received great hospitality and kindness from Lady Gregory.

41] *We were the last romantics:* Yeats' elegy for what he and Lady Gregory have championed in their lives and their art. Yeats writes of Lady Gregory: 'She had made the people a part of her soul; a phrase of Aristotle's had become her motto, "To think like a wise man, but to express oneself like the common people."' This was their shared enterprise on the 'high horse' (Pegasus) of poetry and drama. The poem comes full circle in the last line with the swan drifting over the now darkening water.

Lapis Lazuli

A lapis lazuli medallion, on which was carved the figure of an old man and his servant, was given to Yeats by Harry Clifton.

1] *hysterical women:* women who reject the 'gaiety' of the arts and choose instead to throw themselves body and soul into politics. This is what Maud Gonne and the Countess Markiewicz had done.

6] *Aeroplane and Zeppelin:* air-raids of the First World War.

7] *Pitch like King Billy bomb-balls in:* William of Orange who used bombs during the Battle of the Boyne in the seventeenth century; as well as the Kaiser, Wilhelm II.

9–24] In this stanza Yeats explores the way the great heroes and heroines of tragedy meet their end. The dread of death gives place to an exultant gaiety. The great tragic moment is also a moment of inexplicable joy and divine illumination.

19] *Black out:* Death, and the moment in the theatre when, the tragedy ended, the curtain falls.

25–36] Like the great tragic heroes, civilizations and the works of the great artists and craftsmen are doomed to perish. The artist knows this; but he also knows that another generation will again create, in the civilization that re-places the one that has perished, other works of art.

29] *Callimachus:* fifth-century Athenian sculptor. Now only one example remains of his work.

36] *And those that build them are gay:* the joy of creation experienced by the artist and craftsman. The reiteration of the word 'gay' is significant. It carries with it in this poem a sense of exquisite beatitude and lightness of heart.

37–56] Yeats moves to the focal point of the poem. The tone now shifts away from the conversational off-hand tone of the beginning to one of quiet dignity and attains 'that placidity which comes from the fullness of con-templative thoughts, the mind not searching but beholding'.

45] *a water-course or an avalanche:* Yeats implies that the interpretation of a work of art, whether poem or stone-carving, lies, to a certain extent, in the eye of the beholder. Yeats implies a similar ambiguity of interpretation in the snow and the petals of the plum and cherry blossom.

53] *One asks for mournful melodies:* the Chinese old men, symbols of the great contemplatives, can face old age, death and the passing of civilizations, like the tragic heroes, with a wrinkled, glittering joy.

An Acre of Grass

1] *Picture and book remain:* Yeats found constant stimulation and enjoyment in pictures as well as reading. His father's and brother's influence may count for a good deal in this respect. (See T. R. Henn, *The Lonely Tower*, ch. 13, 'Painter and Poet'.)

2] *An acre of green grass:* Riversdale, Rathfarnham, Co. Dublin, was Yeats' home from 1932 until his death—although he spent much time abroad.

7] *My temptation is quiet:* Yeats is no longer at the mercy of physical desire.

10] *the mill of the mind:* it is likely that there may be a memory of Blake's 'satanic mills' here. The mind, seen in terms of metaphor, is endowed with a kind of non-human, irresistible power.

11] *Consuming its rag and bone:* cf. 'The Circus Animals' Desertion':

'I must lie down where all the ladders start,
In the foul rag-and-bone shop of the heart.'

24] *An old man's eagle mind:* the metaphor of the eagle, symbol of vigorous aspiring power, contrasts magnificently with the tranquillity and sense of quiet resignation in the opening stanza.

Beautiful Lofty Things

This poem achieves its force by the juxtaposition of recollected memories of Yeats' friends and acquaintances, each 'caught' in a moment of splendid defiance or vivid heroic beauty. The economy of presentation enhances the feeling of resilient vitality.

1] *O'Leary:* John O'Leary (1830–1907), a leader of the Fenian movement. 'My hostess was Ellen O'Leary who kept house for her brother John O'Leary, the Fenian, the handsomest old man I had ever seen...I found sister and brother alike were of Plutarch's people', *Autobiographies,* pp. 94–5.

2] *My father:* John Butler Yeats (1839–1922). After the production of Synge's *The Playboy of the Western World* had brought about a week of rioting in the theatre, Yeats threw open the theatre for a discussion of the play. Yeats took the platform in full evening dress and faced the crowd. His chief supporter was his father.

5] *Standish O'Grady:*

'Towards the end of the evening, when everybody was more or less drunk, O'Grady spoke. He was very drunk, but neither his voice nor his manner showed it. I had never heard him speak, and at first he reminded me of Cardinal Manning. There was the same simplicity, the same gentleness. He stood between two tables, touching one or the other for support, and said in a low, penetrating voice: 'We have now a literary movement, it is not very important; it will be followed by a political movement, that will not be very important; then will come a military movement, that will be important indeed.'

Autobiographies, pp. 423–4

7] *Augusta Gregory:* Lady Gregory told Yeats of this threat to her life at the time of the Irish 'Troubles'. She was about seventy at the time. Yeats makes her courage appear the more impressive by adding another ten years to her age.

10] *Maud Gonne:* a memory of her when she came to Howth where Yeats lived as a young man. It is characteristic that the metaphor, Pallas Athene, is reserved for her: in addition, the metaphor crowns the poem and makes the transition to 'All the Olympians' as easy as it is inevitable.

High Talk

Yeats asserts the rôle of the artist in our degenerate time, his need to be extravagant, 'on high stilts'. The rhythm, at once jaunty and forceful, testifies to the poet's joy in defiance; his flamboyancy; his conviction that a commonplace naturalism is boring, lacking as it all too frequently does, the quality that 'catches the eye'. He, by becoming metaphorically 'heightened', a Stilt-Jack of a performer, will make his audience, like a circus crowd, gape with joy and admiring wonder.

In the second stanza the poem surges to a remarkable climax. The clattering, colloquial words and rhythms give rise to the metaphor of the barnacle goose, at once ridiculous and heroic, flying alone—and in this, like the artist-clown transfigured, larger than life—through the 'terrible novelty of light'. The artist's loneliness at the moment of illumination is perfectly symbolized. Not for nothing have the shrieking women at the end of the first stanza been superseded by the great sea-horses and their marvellous laughter.

The Circus Animals' Desertion

6] *My circus animals:* Yeats' mocking metaphor for the personae of his poems. T. R. Henn suggests that the idea of the circus animals may have sprung from a recollection of his brothers' drawings of horses, riders and circuses which he made for the Cuala Press Broadsheets. The circus was a favourite theme for painting in the last years of the nineteenth and the early twentieth century—as the work of Toulouse-Lautrec, Picasso and Rouault bears witness.

7] *Those stilted boys:* performers in the circus as well as the companions of Yeats in the 'nineties— 'companions of the Cheshire Cheese'. See also the poem 'High Talk' which offers the most satisfying gloss on this epithet.

that burnished chariot: the circus chariot—(there is a painting by Jack Yeats of a superb silvery white chariot)—but Yeats may have Cuchulain's chariot in mind.

8] *Lion and woman:* the sphinx, familar motif of Yeats and other artists in the 'nineties, cf. Wilde, Shannon.

9] *old themes:* the poems that Yeats wrote before he met Maud Gonne in 1889—in particular *The Wanderings of Oisin.*

10] *Oisin:* a chivalric Irish mythological hero.

led by the nose: Niamh made advances to Oisin because he was too chivalrous to ask her for her love. Niamh means 'man-picker'. The blending of the common idiom ('led by the nose' and 'the Lord knows what') with the language of higher dignity is carried off with superb skill.

15–16] The connection between the poet's life and art is touched upon. Niamh is identified with Maud Gonne.

21] *my dear:* Maud Gonne. She acted with great success in his play *Cathleen ni Houlihan.* Her life was wholly devoted to the cause of Irish Nationalism.

25–6] In Yeats' play *On Baile's Strand* (1903), Cuchulain dies fighting the waves—a symbol maybe of the dreamer attempting to hold back the incoming tide of reality. The Fool and the Blind Man are also from this play.

27] *Heart-mysteries there:* Jeffares suggests that the 'heart-mysteries' probably refer to Yeats' life after Maud Gonne married John Macbride.

28–30] Yeats refers to the years of labour that he gave to embody the heroic actions of his legendary characters in his plays and poems—particularly his plays.

31–2] The sheer 'doing' (to use James' word) of the plays; writing them, arranging for them to be acted, supervising rehearsals, etc., seems to cut across devotion to the 'dream'. This poem should be read in conjunction with a much earlier poem 'The Fascination of What's Difficult'.

33–40] Yeats examines the source of his 'masterful images' and states that they are generated out of the chaos of the despised and commonplace—less than that—junk. An analogy may be found in, say, the mess and litter of a property room in a theatre which is 'transformed' when it is used in the performance of a play. The uncompromising list of objects has a fierce metaphoric force that culminates powerfully and startlingly in the final line of the poem. The 'heart' mentioned in each verse of the poem but verse III has not been seen in this context before, which ends the poem on a dis-enchanted ironical thrust.

The Man and the Echo

1] *In a cleft that's christened Alt:* Alt, a rocky fissure on the side of Ben Bulben, serves for Yeats as kind of Irish Delphi. The sense of its being a holy place is conveyed by 'christened'.

6–10] Yeats, aware of his approaching death, seeks to know the meaning and purpose of his life and work. Questions about his responsibility as an artist and a human being torment and perplex him for, at this oracle, question must serve as answer.

11–12] The play is *Cathleen ni Houlihan* which was performed in Dublin in 1902. Maud Gonne played the name part with such compelling beauty and passion that the effect on the audience was dynamic.

13–14] Yeats apparently criticized certain Margot Ruddock's poems. He wonders if this has been a contributory cause of her madness.

15–16] Yeats ponders if his intervention could have prevented Coole Park from being destroyed.

17–19] Action or the lack of it seems equally to end in failure or evil. Hence the despairing echo. But this is instantly rejected.

19–36] Yeats knows that there is no satisfaction to be had from capitulation. He accepts the need for 'effort and expectation and desire' throughout life, the need at the brink of death to stand in judgement on the soul before 'the night'.

37 et seq.] The meditation on the nature of death—whether he will rejoice or not when death takes place—is harshly interrupted by the death anguish of the rabbit. The rabbit's scream cuts across the answer to Yeats' question which, following the line of poem, implies the echoed 'Rejoice'. (See also 'Lapis Lazuli', stanza II).

EDWARD THOMAS

The Owl

Edward Thomas' poetry is always characterized by the quiet cadence of the speaking voice. His poems are usually built upon contrasts which point to the essential isolation of the living creature, or of man, in the natural order. Thus, in this poem, warmth and shelter and the company of men (which he loved) are qualified by the cry of the owl of which he wrote 'Beautiful as their notes are for their quality and order, it is their inhumanity that gives them their greatest fascination, the mysterious sense that they bear to us that the earth is something more than a human estate...'. Here, as elsewhere, is found that 'bitter salting of the palate of human experience' of which Mr Coombes has spoken in his book on Thomas.

Swedes

Another contrast, this time between the idea of life in death, the continuity of the natural rhythm, and the finality of the death of man in his tomb. The irony and the affirmation, prefaced by the words 'tender-gorgeous', are caught up in the two closing lines. Note the security and strength of the blank verse despite its quiet, almost casual, tone. Note, too, the precision with which the observation is made. Thomas had perhaps the best eye and ear of his generation of poets; but the accuracy of his descriptions is deeply and inwardly felt. They bespeak what F. R. Leavis has called 'The inner life which the sensory impressions are notation for'.

11] *Amen-hotep:* an Egyptian King of the eighteenth Dynasty.

October

This poem discovers the fidelity not only of Thomas' observation but also of his thought and feeling. The phrase 'The rich scene' is entirely justified not merely by the sense for and the detail of his landscape, but by the way in which the scene is touched and pointed by his own sense of desolation and apartness (lines 12 et seq.).

He presents landscape as vividly as a pictorial artist, and constantly modifies it by his own mood or attitude. He is concerned with states of being rather than with a simple record of things seen.

The control of rhythm, intonation, and cadence in his blank verse is exemplified throughout the poem. For example, in the falling cadence of the second line the 'l' and 's' sounds counterpoint the assertive consonants of the first line which is emblazoned by the great bough of gold. These sounds slow and check the line until the counterpoint of sound and movement exactly catches the modulation of mood.

Ambition

The mood of the preceding poem is more poignantly caught here. The poem elucidates the meaning of things seen; the contrast, for example, between the Tamburlaine-like vitality and defiance of the jackdaw or the mocking laughter of the woodpecker, and the echoing and sombre unease of the owl's cry. The windy spaces between earth and sky seem often to point to the alienation between two spheres of being, an experience reinforced by contrasting images of light and dark, movement and stillness, life and death. These are the framework of human experience in the immediate present. Human ambition can only anchor itself to the present—as here where the moment of stillness, a perception of bliss, is quickly betrayed by the revelation of the transience of busy and energetic life.

Sedge-warblers

Thomas knew the dangers of a merely literary response to Nature; the way in which they can lead to an attractive but false myth-making, a condition of dream—long past and irrecoverable—of which he speaks in the first paragraph of this poem. The dream, rejected, gives way to the unsentimental and accurate response of the second part of the poem. The song must be truthful—quick, shrill, or grating. Things speak truth if one hears them aright. There is always this refusal to be deluded, a rejection of romantic idealization and the comforting acceptance of the cosiness of one's own experience. In 'The Chalk Pit' the same attitude to life is expressed.

The control of rhythm and rhyme patterns in this poem is notable; for example, the way in which the confident intonation commanded by the rising stress on 'unstained' in the eighth line finds its appropriate, but delayed, response in the line with which, in the second paragraph, it seeps slowly away through the rejecting consonants and end rhyme 'drained'.

Liberty

Alone, with the moon in the cold frost of the last light (the contiguity of light and dark is stressed again), the poet and the moon, the remaining points of consciousness, think of the buried past and reflect nostalgically upon an idea of freedom which the second part of the poem immediately rejects. Thomas cannot and will not escape the life of which he is himself a part; memory is a useless support. The inversion of Keats is telling—Thomas moves towards life: 'I still am half in love with pain'

Its darkness is accepted, the cold serenity of the moon acknowledged and dismissed.

5] 'Unforgotten' is used here curiously. It has not the sense of 'held in the memory', but rather that, having no existence, 'everything else' has never had any place in memory. The poem turns on a major contrast: the pain and the pleasure of the present set against a past so remote that memory cannot quicken to it, and a future so uncertain that the mind recoils from it.

Old Man

This is a poem about names and things and their relation to man in time. The very distinction between the names proposes a time-theme reinforced by rosemary (for remembrance) and lavender (in which things are laid for future use). The herb itself sharpens the sense of the present and, at the same time, defines the isolation of man even within his home. Its qualities, in the second paragraph, quicken a detailed and loving particularization of the present; man and child, the ordered domestic scene: yet these are, as we discover in the two concluding paragraphs, nullified by the necessary bitter odour as it enforces the final disconsolate sense of disorientation and the elusive nature of experience. But the poem is as important for what it affirms as for what it seems to deny. It begins with a name: it concludes with the word 'nameless' which has gained force from what has gone before. Thomas's care for language is finely exemplified in this poem, a concern defined, perhaps, by a comment in his book on Pater: 'Only when a word has become necessary to him can a man use it safely; if he tries to impress words by force on a sudden occasion, they will either perish of his violence or betray him.'

As the Team's Head-brass

The commonplace elements of this poem are bound together into a statement of strength and maturity by the sweetness and inclusiveness of Thomas' observation. It is a fine poem not least because of the way in which it provides an authentic sense of the poet's own presence. The variation of rhythm and the counterpointing of word, phrase, line and conversation, the apparently casual manner concealing the firm control over the blank verse that comes as near to good prose as it dare without ever losing its momentum; these are all factors that make it memorable.

The opening line with its heavy rhythm marries the movement of horse and plough to the flash of light (itself a kind of revelation) which illuminates the disappearing lovers. The human agents are as much a part of the natural order as the field, the wood, and the fallen elm. Thomas proposes a continuity in this poem that seems often to elude him in other moods, other poems. The appropriateness of 'strewed', the resonance of 'treading me down', the juxtaposition of 'About the weather' and 'next about the war' are all keys to a reading of the poem.

An identity is established not merely between the death of the tree and the death of the ploughman: the regular rhythm of 'one minute and an interval of ten' widens imperceptibly into a larger rhythm reinforced by the departing and returning lovers, by the meditative conversation, and by the firm relation of man to nature in the three concluding lines. Love, fertility, life, and death are all comprehended in this poem.

Lights Out

The image of the forest stands often for self-immolation in sleep or in death in Thomas' poetry. This poem, then, contemplates death; but the positive assertion noted in 'Liberty' is still implicit: 'I still am half in love with pain, / With what is imperfect'. He, the imperfect, is one of the 'things that have an end' but the poem celebrates these things even while it moves away from them. Life is not denied in the irrevocable movement towards silence.

Cock-crow

It is proper to end with a brief poem which may seem slight but is masterly. Thomas plays brilliantly with images—'the wood of thoughts' and 'the sharp axe of light', allows them to grow in the five central lines into a heroic posture and then cuts them down himself, sharply, as he returns in the last line to the world of valued actuality which is his proper poetic claim.

WALTER DE LA MARE

They Told Me

1] *Pan:* the Greek goat-footed god of flocks and shepherds. He invented and played upon musical pipes which he named Syrinx after the nymph he loved who was changed into a reed to escape his love. Plutarch tells us that, in the reign of the Emperor Tiberius, a ship with passengers was driven near the coast of the isles of Paxi. A loud voice was heard calling to Thamous that the Great God Pan was dead.

6] *charged:* both 'accused of' in the sense of 'charged in a court of law with the crime of sorcery', and 'loaded, made rich with'.

All that's Past

The repetition-with-a-difference of the ideas underlying each stanza avoids monotony by the subtle changes of cadence, by the patterning of vowel- and consonant-sounds and by the aura of suggestiveness in the words themselves.

24] *amaranth:* imaginary unfading flower of a purple colour.

Fare Well

The acceptance of death in terms of the gentlest dissolution urges the question of what is permanent in this world's beauty. The lyrical ease mediates between the awareness of beauty lost with the extinguishing of the senses and the trust in beauty's renewal.

6] *the very proof of me:* in one sense, 'the proof of my existence' (because as long as I live I shall feel this wonder) and 'proof' in the technical sense: a testing, a guarantee of quality.

14] *Traveller's Joy:* a hedgerow plant, also called 'Old Man's Beard' (wild clematis).

Gold

The fabulous beauty of some scornful mythical queen whose golden hair is rarer than any gold to be found on earth or in the seas has passed away, along with her palace, now the haunt of birds and overgrown with weeds. Only the wind and the whispering gold of the wheat remain, the latter perennially renewed, playing at their game of courtship.

The swift juxtaposition of contrasting images in word movements that evoke the wind's sound in transit is done with the same sureness of control that contrives the irony and onomatopoeia of the last two lines.

9] *Archiac:* Archias was a Corinthian, descended from Hercules. He founded Syracuse in 732 B.C. Being told by the oracle to make a choice between health and riches, he chose the latter. Presumably this is the person whom the poet has in mind.

I Sit Alone

The world of transient fantasy offers the briefest of respites from the horror of life, the fear of death and the sense of isolation. It is only faith and love that can redeem the condition of time.

Arabia

In a penetrating criticism of Walter de la Mare's poetry, published in *Countries of the Mind*, John Middleton Murry writes:

'But if this opposition of the ideal and the real is one of the great essential themes of poetry, it is also one which yields most to the impress of the poet's personality. Between the one pole of a complete belief in the existence of a kingdom of eternal beauty and imperishable perfection, and the other of an unfaltering recognition that these beatitudes exist in and for the soul alone, are infinite possibilities of faith and doubt, inexhaustible opportunities for the creative activity of art. For, apart from the precise mixture of certainty and hesitation in the poet's mind, one of the sovereign gestures of art is to make the ideal real, and to project a dim personal awareness on to a structure of definite inventions. The sense that we are exiled from our own country, that our right-ful heritage has been usurped from us, we know not how, may impel one poet to create his kingdom in words and name it with names, people it with fit inhabitants, and another to record the bare fact of his consciousness as a homeless wanderer.

Mr. de la Mare is a poet of the great theme who is distinguished chiefly by his faculty of pressing invention and fancy to the service of his need. He has named his other kingdom with many names: it is Arabia; Tartary; Alulvan, or Thule. Within its shifting frontiers are comprised all the dim, debatable lands that lie between the Never-Never country of nursery rhyme and the more solid fields to which the city mind turns for its paradise, the terrestrial happiness which only a shake of the gods' dice-box has denied.'

Music

This poem is included here as something of a period piece whose imagery has affinities with Pre-Raphaelite painting in its last phases and even Art Nouveau.

Maerchen (Fairy Tale)

Elements of fairy tale and folk-proverb conjoin with sharply delineated concrete details. Together they give the remote and dreamlike an unusual immediacy (e.g. the mimetic syncopated bounce of the first line of the second stanza).

De la Mare is here mocking his own tendencies. The third line of each verse is just a little too heavily charged to be serious. The refrain gives the game finally away.

The Ghost

The poet's treatment of the *revenant* theme (a favourite topic) might be compared with certain ballads (e.g. 'Clerk Saunders') or with Hardy's poems 'The Voice' and 'After a Journey': or the nightmare episode in *Wuthering Heights* where the ghost of Catherine Earnshaw appears to Mr Lockwood.

The Children of Stare

The atmosphere of vacant, brooding hostility, frozen silence, a harshness of weather, place and spirit, encompasses but fails to extinguish the persistent warmth and vitality of the children. In this winter world whose only touch of colour is in the redness of the setting sun and the berries, they have a strength, tenuous but real, whose source is divine.

2] *house of Stare:* 'Stare' suggests a hollow-eyed vacancy, the very anti-thesis of the warmth and comfort of home. There is a possible overtone of W. B. Yeats' 'Come Build in the Empty House of the Stare'. In Yeats' poem, the stare is Elizabethan English, as well as Irish, for starling.

4] *its ancestral box:* there is an ambiguity here. The box could be the box hedges to be found in old gardens. Box takes generations to come to maturity. It could be (and is more likely) a reference to an old hunting lodge or shooting box. Understood in this way, the word carries with it the feeling of emptiness, hollowness.

The Song of the Mad Prince

If this is Hamlet's song, it is also de la Mare's. 'She' might be Ophelia, but she is also all dead loves. The loss of the loved one is poignantly conveyed with characteristic lyric tact and grace which solaces without any hint of cloying intrusion. The girl's death is set in a context of the seasonal activities of country life in their tenderest aspects. The riddling world of unanswered questions resolves itself in the sad acceptance implicit in the last four lines.

10] *willow:* the emblem of those who die for love.

The Old Summerhouse

All de la Mare's houses are haunted by ghosts of people, or memories; this, though a summerhouse, is no exception. From its doorway the poet, with the emblems of mortality about him—'dead leaf, like the ghost of a mouse'—hears in the sound of the waterfall the ominous change that attends on natural beauty. The poet's haunted melancholy is reflected in the meditative movement and echoing repetitions of the words and their pleasingly sombre harmonies.

Tom's Angel

One of de la Mare's talents was his ability to write convincingly of that ex-perience of childhood where the supernatural reveals itself disquietingly in the midst of commonplace, day-to-day existence. The street-ballad form and measure, with its appropriately direct language, accommodates itself both to the children and to the 'Angel blue as fire', with his 'bristling' wings. The climactic 'And I saw his hair' communicates the uncanny nearness of the terror so that it takes the turn of both lane and mill wheel in the last stanza before the children find themselves safe in the familiar reality. But—the poem bears witness to it—the revelation *remains*.

John Mouldy

De la Mare evokes the macabre by disarmingly simple means: by repetition of phrase-structure and stanza, and a matter-of fact precision of detail. The 'Dog-Star' with its associations of heat, fever and pestilence and the frighteningly specific 'slim brown rat of Norway' bring the poem to its climax of horror and give a weight of menace to the repeated final stanza.

In both this poem and 'Tom's Angel', de la Mare makes sophisticated use of the superficially innocuous nursery-rhyme elements. This poem springs off from 'I spy with my little eye'. In 'Tom's Angel', Polly Flint is likely to be either ancestor or descendant of Polly Flinders.

An Epitaph

The economy of presentation of the theme—the transience of earthly beauty—is delicately achieved. The lady is just sufficiently specified—'of the West Country'—for her to be at once real and remote. The context of the gentle sprightliness of the second line endows it with poignancy.

In the second stanza, the brevity of haunting phrase vouches for the sense of loss. The unflinching earthiness of 'crumble' sets the seal on a sense of evanescence.

D.H.LAWRENCE

As Lawrence's poetic style matured he moved away from rhyming verses and a fixed formal pattern, to the unrhymed, more flexible movement of free verse, because he felt that by using this means he could explore, and register more accurately and intimately, the contour of the experience. Formal verse made for the fixity of perfection: it was crystalline, permanent with the beauty of the gem.

'This completeness, this consummateness, the finality and the perfection are conveyed in exquisite form: the perfect symmetry, the rhythm which returns upon itself like a dance where the hands link and loosen and link for the supreme moment of the end.'

Instead of this, he wanted to write poetry of the 'immediate present', 'poetry whose very permanency lies in its wind-like transit', 'the quick of all change, and haste and opposition'. Hence the choice of the medium of free verse.

'In free verse we look for the insurgent naked throb of the instant moment. To break the lovely form of metrical verse, and to dish up the fragments as a new substance called vers libre, this is what most free-versifiers accomplish. They do not know that free verse has its own *nature*, that it is neither star nor pearl, but instantaneous like plasm...The utterance is like a spasm, naked contact with all influences at once. It does not want to get anywhere. It just takes place.

For such utterances any externally applied law would be mere shackles and death. The law must come new each time from within.'

That last sentence is important. What distinguishes Lawrence's free verse poems is their absolute fidelity to the flux of the experience, controlled and shaped by the intelligence working at its profoundest levels.

The tone of all the poems from *Birds*, *Beasts and Flowers* (published 1923) (see pp. 72–80) is akin to that of the speaking voice. There is nothing forced about the language which moves with ease and assurance from conversational day-to-day ordinariness—even the flatness of the botanical textbook:

'So many fruits come from roses'

to the exploratory, mimetic length of the following:

'And on the margin, man soft-footed and pristine,
Still, and sensitive, and active,
Audile, tactile sensitiveness as of a tendril that orientates and reaches out,
Reaching out and grasping by an instinct more delicate than the moon's as
　　she feels for the tides.'

The subtle adjustment of line length to meaning; the flow and arrest of
the movement of the words; the stress and relaxation of the rhythm as it points
the nuances of implication: all these demand a finely attuned ear if the reader
is to appreciate the quality of Lawrence's free-verse poetry.

Discord in Childhood

Compare this passage from *Sons and Lovers* with the poem.

'When William was growing up, the family moved from the Bottoms to a
house on the brow of the hill, commanding a view of the valley, which spread
out like a convex cockle-shell, or a clamp-shell, before it. In front of the
house was a huge old ash-tree. The west wind, sweeping from Derbyshire,
caught the houses with full force, and the tree shrieked again. Morel liked it.
"It's music," he said. "It sends me to sleep." But Paul and Arthur and
Annie hated it. To Paul it became almost a demoniacal noise. The winter of
their first year in the new house their father was very bad. The children
played in the street, on the brim of the wide, dark valley, until eight o'clock.
Then they went to bed. Their mother sat sewing below. Having such a
great space in front of the house gave the children a feeling of night, of
vastness and of terror. This terror came in from the shrieking of the tree and
the anguish of the home discord. Often Paul would wake up, after he had
been asleep a long time, aware of thuds downstairs. Instantly he was wide
awake. Then he heard the booming shouts of his father, come home nearly
drunk, then the sharp replies of his mother, then the bang, bang of his father's
fist on the table, and the nasty, snarling shout as the man's voice got higher.
And then the whole was drowned in a piercing medley of shrieks and cries
from the great, wind-swept ash-tree. The children lay silent in suspense,
waiting for a lull in the wind to hear what their father was doing. He might
hit their mother again. There was a feeling of horror, a kind of bristling in the
darkness, and a sense of blood. They lay with their hearts in the grip of an
intense anguish. The wind came through the tree fiercer and fiercer. All the
cords of the great harp hummed, whistled and shrieked. And then came the
horror of the sudden silence, silence everywhere, outside and downstairs.
What was it? Was it a silence of blood? What had he done? The children lay
and breathed the darkness...'

Last Lesson in the Afternoon

This poem, born of irritation and fatigue, registers in its forthright colloquial
language and rhythmic pressure the taut nerves of the teacher at the end of
the day. The intensity of feeling seems about to spill over at any moment;
yet it is just held in check by demands of the form.

Sorrow

See chapters 14 and 15 of *Sons and Lovers*.

The short drifting lines and the swaying hesitant rhythm re-create the feeling of close personal loss. The rhyme is not intrusive—the fidelity to the emotion prevents it from being so. Yet it is just sufficient to suggest some sort of hard-won assurance in the face of the pain of recollection. But even this goes in the broken rhythm and imperfect rhyme of the last line which acts out in its concrete suggestiveness the hairs (like the smoke of the first stanza) drifting up the chimney; life itself drifting into the darkness of death.

8] *her soft-foot malady:* a metaphor for the stealthy and unobtrusive onset of the cancer that his mother died of.

Ballad of Another Ophelia

This is the least subjective (in a biographical sense) of the poems in this section. Probably it is the most successful. Lawrence himself thought highly of it. 'Why, oh why, do you want to cut off the tail of poor "Ophelia's" ballad?' he wrote in protest to Harriet Monroe to whom he had submitted it for publication; and continues:

'Don't you see the poor thing is cracked, and she used all those verses— apples and chickens and rat—according to true instinctive or *dream* symbolism? This poem—I am very proud of it—has got the quality of a troublesome dream that seems incoherent but is selected by another sort of consciousness. The latter part is the waking up part, yet never really awake, because she is mad. No, you mustn't cut it in two. It is a good poem: I couldn't do it again to save my life. Use it whole or not at all...'
                                                                Letters, p. 288

Grapes

Lawrence sees the grape—or rather the vine—as the 'rose' of the early world, before man had become corrupted as a consequence of forced mental activity which overdeveloped his reason at the price of his non-mental 'awareness' and spontaneity.

The Mosquito

The mosquito, like the bat, at once fascinates and repels Lawrence. His ability to feel and express the insect's identity, its lightness, its delicate elegance of shape and substance ('Monsieur') as well as its repulsiveness ('Ghoul on wings...You speck') is powerfully communicated to the reader by subtle shifts of tone and irony.

'He seemed to know', Aldous Huxley wrote in his preface to the *Collected Letters* (1932), 'what it was like to be a tree or a daisy, or a breaking wave, or even the mysterious moon itself. He could get inside the skin of an animal and tell you in the most convincing detail how it felt and how, dimly, inhumanly, it thought.'

38] *trump:* trumpet.

Humming bird

The quotation from Aldous Huxley's preface is relevant to this poem with its economical but suggestive evocation of the primeval world: the thick inarticulacy, and cumbrous movement of elemental vegetable forms against which is played off the scintillating, darting flight of the humming bird, suggested by the thin, flickering assonance. The poem turns about on itself in the last two verses. It is the notion continued in these two 'stanzas' which sets the seal, as it were, on Lawrence's empathetic presentation of the humming bird.

Kangaroo

The feeling for the weight and equipoise, the line and movement of the kangaroo comes across to the reader as if it were a preternaturally strong instinct springing from Lawrence's intuitional energy. Albert Schweitzer's guiding phrase 'reverence for life' might serve as an epigraph for this poem and Lawrence's work in general.

Mountain Lion

Note Lawrence's dramatic use of line length: the opening lines lengthen by a mounting series of brief vivid clauses which are followed by a sudden contraction, full of apprehension and misgiving, as the poet and his companion glimpse the Mexicans. Always the line contracts and the tone becomes curt and edgy when human beings are involved: whereas it undulates and pro- liferates as the animals are felt after.

The poem then opens out into a kind of threnody for the dead lion, a lament for the vigour, the leaping vitality and the beauty which will never again return to the killed creature. As he climbs up into the 'dark valley mouth' to the lion's lair, his identification with the lion's 'situation'—animal beauty and power facing a white, cold, hostile world—becomes more complete until it is broken in the last four lines with an upsurge of sharp anger and sharper regret.

16] *Qué tiene, amigo?:* what have you got there, friend?
17] *León:* a lion.
31] *Hermoso es!:* what a beauty!

Swan

See Yeats' poem, 'Leda and the Swan', on p. 37 for contrast.

Things Men Have Made

See *Women in Love*, chapter XXVI, 'A Chair'. In a review of Eric Gill's *Art Nonsense and other Essays*, Lawrence writes:

'The god who enters us and imbues us with his strength and glory and might and honour and beauty and wisdom, this is the god we are eager to worship. And this is the god of the craftsman who makes things well, so that the presence of the god enters into the things made. The workman making a pair of shoes with happy absorption in skill is imbued with the god of strength and honour and beauty, undeniable. Happy intense absorption in work, which is to be brought as near to perfection as possible, this is the state of being with God and the men who have not known it have missed life itself.'   (*Phoenix*)

To Women, as far as I'm Concerned

The cumulative definitions of what integrity of feeling consists in, lead up forcefully to the last line where 'idea' carries the whole weight of the verse behind it.

Bavarian Gentians/Shadows

Lawrence's sense of his impending death pervades both themes and rhythms of his *Last Poems*. The stridency and carping which marred a number of the poems in *Pansies* and *Nettles* are replaced by a gravely serene dignity of utterance as the life process is taken over by death. Yet even here the emphasis falls on life, on living, on the continual flux of existence. The Bavarian gentians lead to the myth of Dis and Persephone which in its turn includes the poet in its blue darkness. In 'Shadows', emphasis falls as much on renewal as on dissolution. The incantatory, ceremonial rhythms of both these poems enhance their atmosphere of ritual mystery.

4] *Pluto:* god of the underworld, the home of the dead.
8] *Dis:* the Roman god of the underworld. Lawrence appears to use the names of Dis and Pluto as interchangeable.
9] *Demeter:* (Her name may mean 'earth-mother' or 'corn-mother'.) Goddess of corn and of agriculture. She was the mother of Persephone.
14] *Persephone:* the goddess daughter of Demeter and Zeus. She was carried off by Pluto while she was picking flowers in the meadows of Enna in Sicily. Pluto took her in his chariot to the underworld, 'the halls of Dis', where she was made queen. She was sought by Demeter but allowed to return to the earth for only six months of the year.

EZRA POUND

'In the "search for oneself", in the search for "sincere self-expression", one gropes, one finds some seeming verity. One says "I am this, that, or the other", and with the words scarcely uttered one ceases to be that thing.

I began this search for the real in a book called *Personae*, casting off, as it were, complete masks of the self in each poem. I continued in a long series of translations, which were but more elaborate masks'

                              Ezra Pound, *Gaudier-Brzeska: A Memoir* (1916)

Apart from the major achievement of *Hugh Selwyn Mauberley*, Ezra Pound's particular distinction lies mainly in his translations, or 'translucencies' as T. S. Eliot has called them, in which Pound has made certain poems of the past viable for the twentieth century. Though scholars have criticized him adversely for his inaccuracies and howlers, the fact remains that Pound has *invented* poetic forms and a poetic language that suggest the mood and tenor of the originals in such a way that a representative group of Anglo-Saxon,

French, Provençal, Italian and Chinese poems are no longer the province of recondite scholarship. They are part of the terrain of modern poetry.

Pound is primarily a poet who has acquired his skill with very great labour. He is as T. S. Eliot has pointed out in the dedication of *The Waste Land*, *il miglior fabbro*, the better craftsman. As a poet he is committed to making a poem: not a crib. The poetic integrity is his chief concern. By means of these translations, Pound finds himself, so to speak, in making new (and here lies his originality) those poems which otherwise would be forgotten in the dust of libraries.

The Return

The subject of this poem (first printed in *The English Review*, June 1912) is hard to define, and is probably meant to be. The more it keeps its mystery, the more potent its suggestiveness. If the objective reality is to be found, it is most readily perceptible in the accomplishment of the poise which springs from Pound's sense of cadence. The poem cannot be dismissed as vague. Or, if one calls it 'vague', it is not the vagueness of incompetence; rather, the unemphatic, tentative rhythms and word-sounds guarantee by their weight and their duration, by the way they are arranged upon the page, a poem whose condition and nature lie closer to music than to poetry. The exhaustion of the once-vigorous hunters, whether they be men or gods or abstract notions made concrete, comes through to the reader by means of the rhythm which interprets this experience with singular expressiveness.

13] *Haie:* the cry of the hunters.
17] *leash-men:* hunters.

The Gipsy

An encounter is traditional material for poetry; Wordsworth's 'Resolution and Independence' and 'Stepping Westward' (particularly the former) are admirable examples of this genre. Pound seems to hint ironically at Arnold in the epigraph; but this gipsy is as far removed from Arnold's arch-escapist as one could wish. A closer parallel with Pound's poem would be Edward Thomas' 'The Chalk Pit' or 'Up in the Wind', where the reverberations attendant upon so slight an experience are implied in the tone and cadence rather than stated explicitly. The poet leaves the reader to formulate the generalization arising from the perfectly realized specific instance (if he must!).

The epigraph in French is translated in lines 2 and 3 of the poem.

8] The reference to Arles and Biaucaire points to Pound's interest in and knowledge of Provençal poetry and the world of the troubadours and jongleurs.

The Seafarer

Shortly after Pound had embarked on a series of translations of Chinese poetry (to be published in 1915 as *Cathay*) he translated the Anglo-Saxon poem, 'The Seafarer' (published 1912 in *Ripostes*). In his *A.B.C. of Reading* (1934/1951) he remarks upon the resemblance in poetic structure between Chinese and Anglo-Saxon poetry:

'I once got a man to start translating "The Seafarer" into Chinese. It came out almost directly as Chinese verse, with two solid ideograms in each half-line. Apart from the "Seafarer" I know no other European poems of the period you can hang up with the "Exile's Letter" of Li Po, displaying the West on a par with the Orient.'

Professor Davie, in *Ezra Pound: Poet as Sculptor*, points out that over and above the awareness of a similarity of structure-pattern in the Anglo-Saxon and Chinese Poems, there is also a similarity of attitude in the personae of the two poems: or, at least Pound endows them with this. In the 'Exile's Letter' there is defiance through indifference to conventional attitudes; in 'The Seafarer' by Pound's eliminating of the conventional Christian elements in the original poem, a defiance by malice of those forces, natural or human, that threaten one's way of life. Through the agency of the Anglo-Saxon and the Chinese masks, Pound enacts his personal situation which, though never obtrusive, is there clearly enough. The seafarer is not the only one dedicated to a task, fulfilling a vocation: Pound is, too—whatever the cost.

Rhythm, not rhyme, governs the structure of Anglo-Saxon poetry: alliteration, rhythmically stressed, forms the unifying pattern within each line of Anglo-Saxon poetry. The lines are often of irregular length; but they are divided along their length by a strongly marked caesura (or pause) falling roughly midway along the line. This allows the alliterative patterning to make itself felt as the element that not only links the second half of the line with the first, but gives expressive emphasis to the line's emotional contour and its onomatopoeic richness. The 'line-unit' of this poetry makes a strong appeal to Pound as can be seen from both 'The Seafarer' and the *Cathay* poems which follow.

Rhythmically, 'The Seafarer' is a *tour de force*. Pound feels for the shape of the line, its pressures and tensions, the stress and emphasis of consonant linkage beating up against the mid-line bulwark of the caesurae. The physicality of such writing justifies Charles Norman's comment that 'Pound's rhythms stride with giant steps and there are great gulps of air, instead of mere caesurae, in the clash of syllables'.

Creating a twentieth-century Anglo-Saxon measure had a liberating influence on the rhythms of English poetry. It necessitated a break from the blank verse line which, by the beginning of the twentieth century, had become exhausted. 'To break the pentameter, that was the first heave' ('Canto 81'). So Pound, in retrospect on his poetic assignment.

Finally, there is a wonderful clarity of image, a sharpness of delineation and an avoidance of abstraction.

2] *jargon:* specialized language to describe a particular vocation or activity.

4] *breast-cares:* heartfelt anxieties and distress.

12] *Mere-weary mood:* a dreariness and heaviness of spirit: a kind of sea-weariness.

17] *hail-scur:* a blast of cutting hailstones.

19] *at whiles:* on occasion, from time to time.

20] *Did:* served as, afforded.

22] *mead-drink:* wine made from fermented honey.

32] *nightshade:* shadow of night.

34] *Nathless:* nevertheless.

37] *lust:* desire.

39] *fastness:* stronghold.

40] *mood-lofty:* exalted in mind and heart.

45] *ring-having:* the exchange of rings in marriage.
46] *winsomeness:* attractiveness, delightfulness.
47] *whit:* tiny portion, bit, least possible amount.
49] *Bosque:* wood, spinney, trees.
50] *land fares brisker:* the earth becomes alive with bursting growth.
59] *breastlock:* locked within the breast (in the ribcage).
60] *mere-flood:* full tide, a flowing sea.
61] *whale's acre:* where the whale lives, the whale's 'land'.
74] *Laud:* praise.
91] *seareth:* withers.
92] *the earth's gait:* at the same pace as the earth.

from *Cathay*: The River-merchant's Wife: a Letter; Lament of the Frontier Guard; Exile's Letter; Taking Leave of a Friend

In his Introduction to Pound's *Selected Poems*, T. S. Eliot says: 'As for *Cathay*, it must be pointed out that Pound is the inventor of Chinese poetry for our time.'

He points out that Pound stands in relation to Chinese poetry as the great Elizabethan translators, Chapman, Florio and North, stood in relation to Homer, Montaigne and Plutarch. These men produced 'magnificent specimens of Tudor prose': Pound has produced in *Cathay* 'a magnificent specimen of twentieth-century poetry' rather than a faultless translation. 'Each generation', Eliot says, 'must translate for itself.'

Pound made his translations after studying the writings of Ernest Fenellosa who had been Imperial Commissioner of Art in Tokyo. Fenellosa saw that English, because it was the least inflected and strongest of European languages, was the most suitable one to use for translation from Chinese. Moreover, the full force and concision of Chinese ideograms find an accommodating syntax in English. This factor accounts for the particular satisfactoriness of the *Cathay* translations, especially when it is moved by such melodically expressive rhythms. The poems *sound* right in the mind's ear. Pound was thus fulfilling the principle he enunciated in 1912 as part of the Imagiste programme by 'composing in the sequence of musical phrase, not in the sequence of a metronome'.

The unit of verse in these poems is the line, which is usually a complete sentence. The linkage of line with line is brought about by parallels, either actual or apparent, in the grammatical structure of each sentence; and, though alliteration occurs as a poetic means of patterning, it more frequently subserves the suggestiveness of the onomatopoeia, for Pound's use of the accepted poetic devices is austerely controlled in the interests of directness and clarity. Though it is true to say that Pound has antecedents for this kind of writing in the Bible, and poets like Christopher Smart and Whitman, this in no way diminishes the poetic subtlety of Pound's *Cathay*.

from *Homage to Sextus Propertius*: IX

Homage to Sextus Propertius was published in 1919, although Pound had written the poem two years before. As its sentiments were not in accord with the mood of England at that time, it would have been tactless for it to appear in 1917. In a letter to the *English Journal* in January 1931, Pound wrote that 'it presents certain emotions vital to me in 1917, faced with the infinite and ineffable imbecility of the British Empire as they were to Propertius some centuries earlier, when faced with the infinite and ineffable stupidity of the Roman Empire. These emotions are defined largely, but not entirely, in Propertius' own terms. If the reader does not find relation to life defined in them, he may conclude I have been unsuccessful in my endeavour.' The *Homage* is not so much a translation as an occasion for writing a poem which testifies to the poet's responsible irresponsibility in the hour of national crisis. It speaks for the private right, the personal predicament, setting their claims forward, in front of the public or national cause.

Part of the extract given in this book had already been translated by Pound as early as 1911:

Prayer for his lady's life

Here let thy clemency, Persephone, hold firm,
Do thou, Pluto, bring here no greater harshness.
So many thousand beauties are gone down to Avernus,
Ye might let one remain above with us.
With you is Iope, with you the white-gleaming Tyro,
With you is Europa and the shameless Pasiphae,
And all the fair from Troy and all from Achaia,
From the sundered realms, of Thebes and of aged Priamus;
And all the maidens of Rome, as many as they were,
They died and the greed of your flame consumes them.

    Here let thy clemency, Persephone, hold firm,
    Do thou, Pluto, bring here no greater harshness.
    So many thousand fair are gone down to Avernus,
    Ye might let one remain above with us.

Comparison of this poem with Pound's later version will clearly show the advance in subtlety of treatment. The cadence in the second version is that much more sure of its contemporary relevance.

1] *rhombs:* a kind of conch.

2] *laurel:* the wreath given to the poet for his achievement. The poet was crowned with this wreath.

5] *Avernus:* the underworld of death.

11] *Persephone and Dis:* the queen and king of the World of the Dead.

13] *Iope:* daughter of Inachus. She was loved by Zeus who changed her into a heifer to conceal her from his wife, Hera.

Tyro: daughter of Salmoneus, loved by Poseidon, who visited her disguised as a river and made a great wave to curl over and conceal them.

Pasiphae: wife of Minos, King of Crete. Minos refused to sacrifice to Poseidon a beautiful bull which he had promised to do. To punish him, Poseidon caused Pasiphae to become enamoured of the bull. She gave birth to a monster, half-bull, half-man, the minotaur.

Achaia = whole of Greece? Latin dict. asserts that this is Propertius' meaning here.

Troad: Troy.

Campania: territory in Italy which included Capua, Naples and Pompeii.

from *Hugh Selwyn Mauberley*: iv 'These fought in any case'; v
'There died a myriad'; Envoi: 'Go, dumb-born book'

These are three poems from the first part of a far longer work which comprises
thirteen poems: there are five poems in the second part of the work. If the
three poems are to make their appropriate impact, they should be studied in
their proper context.

When considering the achievement of *Hugh Selwyn Mauberley*, one might
adapt Pound's remark about Hardy's poetry ('Here is the harvest of the
novels') to something like 'Here is the harvest of the translations'—because
in this poem sequence, Pound's steadily acquired flexibility of technique is
exploited with maximum power. By common critical consent *Hugh Selwyn
Mauberley* is Pound's original masterpiece *technically*. But it is more than
that: it creates in its variety of modes, its shifts of tone and meaningful
juxtaposition which bring a range of irony into play, the cultural predicament
of contemporary civilization in terms of poetic myth. (The final chapters of
Lawrence's *Women in Love* give a comparable exploration in fiction of a
similar situation.)

Hugh Selwyn Mauberley is a poet, a latter-day aesthete (and here the poet
is representative of any kind of artist) who finds himself able to make nothing
but the slightest and most tentative contribution to the cultural life of his
time. The social and cultural traditions which have nourished him no longer
have meaning. The values which he seeks to embody in his art are drained of
significance. The refined but tenuous poetic resources which he has at his
command are 'out of key' with his time which values the shoddy, the second-
rate and the mechanical. The poet's predicament is part of a wider and more
tragic predicament whose climax is the calamity of modern war.

The first two poems in this selection deal with the Great War (1914–18).
They are quite unlike the work of other war poets in their detached presentation of the war situation. Pound models his measures on those of the late-
Greek pastoral poet, Bion, with extraordinary effect. The old measure is made
new in the numbed rhythms, the employment of intermittent rhymes, sound-
echoes and similar phrase-shapes which turn back on themselves with irony
and pathos. In the second of these poems, Pound seems to call bitterly into
question the values of art and literature on which he has set such store, by
weighing the loss of the myriad of men, killed in battle, against the value of
works of art. The incisiveness of the poem is not blunted by abstraction: it
makes its point through its terseness and the concreteness of its contrasts.
Hence, the goddess of civilization is a bitch with rotten teeth, senile, yet
potent in her demand for allegiance to her books, now battered, and her
broken statues. Her physical attribute of rotten teeth is contrasted by implication with the physical attributes of the dead young men, the eyes and
good mouth, organs of the vital senses of sight and taste which will never
taste and see again, shut down as they are under the *lid* of the earth.

The Latin tag employed sardonically by Pound is 'Dulce et decorum est
pro patria mori'. 'It is sweet and fitting to die for one's country.'

The 'Envoi' stands between the first part of *Hugh Selwyn Mauberley* and
the second. Although thematically it has its place in the total design it is

different in tone and movement from what has gone before and comes afterwards. In all the printed *complete* versions of *Hugh Selwyn Mauberley* the 'Envoi' is set in italics, which serves to distinguish the 'Envoi', to 'set it off' not merely decoratively (for Pound always seeks to use typography meaningfully). This poem is Pound's farewell to an England grown heedless, even indifferent, to a cultural tradition which had existed most richly at the beginning of the seventeenth century and had nourished and sustained the arts of poetry and music: Henry Lawes' music for the poems of Edmund Waller (and for Milton's songs in the masque of *Comus*). Here, the melody of sound and gravity of pace serve to create the object of their elegy. But the real impact of the poem is made by Pound's sensitive use of tragic parody: he employs a verse form and movement that keep Edmund Waller's poem 'Go, lovely Rose' haunting the mind at the same time as one reads the poem. The delicate plangency of this cantabile movement enhances the poignancy of the theme, especially at those moments when Pound moves out beyond the limits of Waller's verse form.

2] *Tell her:* tell England.

Lawes: Henry Lawes (1596–1662) was a Gentleman of Charles I's Chapel Royal. He composed the music for *Comus* and also for Herrick's Christmas songs in *Hesperides*. Milton addressed this sonnet to him:

> 'Harry, whose tuneful and well-measured song
> First taught our English music how to span
> Words with just note and accent...'

The significance of such an achievement for Pound is obvious.

23] *our two dusts:* the dust of the poet and his book.

Waller's: Edmund Waller (1606–87). He showed a marked precocity as a poet, using heroic couplets as early as 1625. He is chiefly to be remembered for the polished simplicity of his poetry of which Dryden thought highly.

Canto II

Readers familiar with the poetic structure of T. S. Eliot's *The Waste Land* will find structural affinities in Pound's *Cantos*: most notably in the poetic collage whereby apparently unrelated scraps of classical myth, ancient legend, esoteric reference and literary allusion are re-organized into a new unity by the poet as a means of exploring his theme. These fragments regarded in their complex totality offer the clue to the theme (and hence the meaning) of the canto. So that, more specifically, the reader needs to grasp what brings together Browning's *Sordello*, Sordello himself and Pound's 'idea' of Sordello, the Chinese Emperor So-Shu, Eleanor of Aquitaine, Helen of Troy, the legend of Tyro and Poseidon and the legend of Acoetes and Bacchus. Browning, *The Iliad, the Odyssey* and Ovid's *Metamorphoses*—particularly the last— are the quarries that Pound works in order to present his theme, which, Hugh Kenner suggests, is 'the artist's struggle to bring form (Browning's *Sordello* and Pound's *Cantos*) out of flux (the Sordello documents, the sea)'. So-Shu, the Chinese Emperor, 'churned in the sea'. Churning is a method of turning fluid into solid. He was also famous for building roads—thus fixing, by construction, a way.

So-Shu's churning in the sea finds its parallel in the legend of Acoetes and Bacchus. The parallelism is just sufficient to satisfy the needs of the theme. The story of the god who brings about the metamorphosis of the sailors (who are impotently churning the waters) and the ship, is another way of concretely presenting the theme of form out of flux in dramatic and mythic terms which are readily apprehended. The final form is, of course, the 'fixing of the story in the poem'.

This is established in the opening line, after its Browningesque parody opening: 'there can be *but the one* "Sordello"'.

In the Tyro myth and the Acoetes story what remains memorable is the stillness that succeeds the movement and turbulence; in the first the 'quiet suntawny sand-stretch', with the gulls and the snipe; in the second, the stone forms as of sculpture washed by the shift of the water:

> 'If you will lean over the rock
>   the coral face under wave-tinge...'

or: 'The swimmer's arms turned to branches',

or, more poignant still:

> 'The smooth brows, seen and half-seen,
> Now ivory stillness.'

Indeed the re-working of the Greek legend of Acoetes is of such brilliance that there is the temptation to bilk the thematic idea in order to respond to the beauty and vigour of the translation, whose rhythms, being so expressive in their sensitivity, vouch for and enhance the reality of the experience and the concreteness of its presentation.

1] '*Sordello*': a poem by Robert Browning written in 1840. Pound tells us that he 'is one of the few people who knew anything about Browning's Sordello'.
3] Sordello came from Mantuan territory.
6] *daughter of Lir:* a moon goddess, marriage to whom confers kingship.
  eyes of Picasso: eyes like those painted by Picasso.
9] *Eleanor:* Eleanor of Aquitaine and Helen of Troy. Eleanor of Aquitaine was married to Louis VII of France when she was thirteen but was divorced fifteen years later on the ground of incompatibility. She then married Henry, Count of Anjou, who became Henry II of England. While her husband was engaged in his quarrel with the Church and Becket, Eleanor was holding court at Poitiers where she presided over the Courts of Love.
  ἑλέναυς: helenaus—destroyer of ships.
  ἑλέπτολις: heleptolis—destroyer of cities. The Homeric-type epithets pun on the names of the two women.
12 et seq.] *Iliad*, Book III:

'At this gate, Priam was sitting in conference with the Elders of the city, Panthous and Thymoetes, Lampus and Clytius, Hicetaon, offshoot of the War-god, and his two wise counsellors, Ucalegon and Antenor. Old age had brought their fighting days to an end, but they were excellent speakers, these Trojan Elders, sitting there on the tower, like cicadas perched on a tree in the woods chirping delightfully. When they saw Helen coming to the tower, they lowered their voices. 'Who on earth,' they asked one another, 'could blame the Trojan and Achaean men-at-arms for suffering so long for such a woman's sake? Indeed, she is the very image of an immortal goddess. All the same, and lovely as she is, let her sail home and not stay here to vex us and our children after us.'

Homer, The Iliad, trans. E. V. Rieu (Penguin Books, 1959)

16] *Schoeney's daughters:* Schoeneus' daughter was Atalanta. (See Ovid, *Metamorphoses*, X, 506–707.)

20 et seq.] The legend of Tyro and Poseidon is recounted in *Odyssey*, Book XI:

'The first I saw was highborn Tyro, who told me she was the daughter of the noble Salmoneus and had married Cretheus, Aeolus' son. She fell in love with the god of the River Enipeus, the loveliest river that runs on earth, and often wandered on the banks of his beautiful stream, until one day the Lord of the Earthquake, the Girdler of the World, disguised himself as the river-god and lay with her where the river rushes out to sea. A dark wave gathered mountain-high, curled over them, and hid the woman and the god. He then unclasped her virgin belt and sealed her eyes in sleep. But when his love had had its way, he took her hand in his; and now he spoke. "Lady," he said, "be happy in this love of ours, and as the year completes its course, since a god's embrace is never fruitless, you will give birth to beautiful children, whom you must nurse and rear with care. But now go home, and guard your tongue. Tell no-one; but I wish you to know that I am Poseidon, the Shaker of the Earth". The god then disappeared under the heaving sea. Tyro conceived, and gave birth to Pelias and Neleus, who both rose to power as servants of almighty Zeus. Pelias lived in the spacious lands of Iolcus, and his wealth lay in his flocks; while Neleus had his home in sandy Pylos. Nor were these the only children of this queen among women. To Cretheus she bore three other sons, Aeson and Pheres and Amythaon, that gallant charioteer.'

Homer, The Odyssey, trans. E. V. Rieu (Penguin Books, 1959)

30 et seq.] The legend of Acoetes, from Book III of Ovid's *Metamorphoses* (see Mary M. Innes' translation, Penguin Books, 1955), may be paraphrased as follows:

Acoetes, captured by Pentheus' slaves, tells his story. His father, a Lydian, left him nothing but his skill as a fisherman. Acoetes soon tired of fishing from the shore, and has become a skilled helmsman.

Under way for Delos he puts in at Chios, where he and his oarsmen spend the night. In the morning the oarsmen return to the boat dragging a young boy whom they have captured as a slave. Acoetes recognizes the boy as more than mortal, and warns his men. They brush aside his protest.

Hoping to deceive the boy, the crew ask him where he would like them to take him. He replies that he wants to go to Naxos. When Acoetes sets sail towards Naxos his crew indicate to him in nods and whispers that he should steer past the island. He refuses to comply, and says that someone else must take the helm. One, Aethalion, takes his place and they pass Naxos.

The god, pretending that he has just noticed their treachery, stands in the stern lamenting. The crew laugh, and row the harder. But the boat stands still. All efforts with oar and sail are of no avail. Ivy twines round the oars, hampering them, and hangs in clusters from the sails. The god reveals himself as Bacchus, his head wreathed with grapes and in his hand a wand draped with vine-leaves. Around him lie phantom shapes of tigers, lynxes and panthers. The oarsmen jump overboard and are turned into porpoises as they leap. Acoetes remains alone on the boat with the god, who tells him to make for Dia's isle. Once there, Acoetes is initiated into the sacred mysteries and becomes a worshipper of Bacchus.

from Canto LXXXI

Throughout the *Cantos* Pound is quick to scourge human pretension and the folly of human behaviour in a tone which is often coarse, bewildering and shrill. In this passage a serener and more authoritative tone prevails that gives the writing a memorable and oracular power. Freed from the dismembered syntax and the abstruse reference which befog the reader in vast tracts of the *Cantos*, this passage is notable for its compassionate restraint. The castigation of human vanity is accomplished with great force through a simplicity and directness of statement which is heightened by the humility and relevance of Pound's reference to the natural world.

2] *reft:* taken away.
16] *Pacquin:* a famous Parisian couturier.
17] *casque:* a helmet.
28] *rathe:* quick.

T.S.ELIOT

The Love Song of J. Alfred Prufrock

The epigraph, a quotation from Dante's *Inferno* (XXVII, 61–6), sets the tone and mood of the poem. Guido da Montefeltro identifies himself thus: 'If I thought that I were answering someone who might return to the world, this flame should shake no more. But since, if I hear truly, no one ever returned alive from this abyss, I have no fear of infamy and answer you.' This sombre comment stands as epigraph to a love song; the love song of a man with an absurd name. A poem about love is, then, to be related to the desolation of Guido. The poem concerns itself with the physical, social, and emotional setting of the problem of love: more simply, it identifies the place, then the problem, and finally the resolution. This is not done in simple sequence: there is a careful interweaving of theme with theme. It may help to read the poem in sections.

Section I: lines 1–14] At the outset of the poem the mood of the epigraph is reinforced with images of sickness and helplessness; the sense that the protagonist is passive rather than vital and active. This is linked, not to Prufrock himself, but to the context of place by which Prufrock is first defined. The meaningless specificity of the epithets reinforces the threatening yet generalized and anonymous location, e.g. 'certain half-deserted streets'.

The adjectives that follow reinforce the general unease, 'muttering', 'restless', 'tedious'; and they, in turn, are reinforced by the sense of disgust embodied in 'one-night cheap hotels' and 'sawdust restaurants'. The time has been established, the place defined, and Prufrock's interior world has been sensed. All of which leads to a question that is deliberately avoided: the visit must be paid, first to the room of lines 13–14.

Section II: lines 15–36] The poem immediately recoils from the room in which the talk is of Michelangelo, the sculptor of the heroic male; recoils into Prufrock's interior world. The conceit which relates fog with cat is not merely a witty exercise, it enables the reader to judge Prufrock because it relates his mental world to these images. Characteristically, the concrete image is used to analyse modes of feeling. The image is physical but its effects are insubstantial; they suggest lethargy and weariness. There is always time, of course, in which the insistent question can be parried, obscured in the prevailing atmosphere of timeless indecision. The word 'time' echoes through these lines: its uses are bitterly remarked once in the incisive line 'To prepare a face to meet the faces that you meet'. All seems obscured in time by the prevailing fog; time culminates only 'to drop a question on your plate'. This is also a kind of inferno, a numbing condition, like social discomfort, to which, as the poem makes clear, it is closely related. Note the way in which the acid comment on self-conscious accommodation to society (line 27) is set against the violent phrase 'murder and create': a flash of violence that sorts oddly with the substitution of one social mask for another. The final incongruity is the moment of the question—tea-time. Then the room is recalled which, characteristically, Prufrock seems not to have visited after all.

Section III: lines 37–48] Prufrock does not take us into the room. It is all in the future, all an assumption based on past experience. These are the recurrent patterns of experience to which he is committed.

> 'Time present and time past
> Are both perhaps present in time future,
> And time future contained in time past.'
>
> 'Burnt Norton'

The time-theme is now linked to Prufrock's fear, 'time / To wonder, "Do I dare?"' He turns back down the stair, another symbol frequently used by Eliot to represent effort, strain or tension; turns back conscious of the stigma of middle age, a bald spot, of the pathetic need to assert himself, to clothe his sense of inadequacy, despite the thinning hair, arms and legs, in sartorial elegance. The mock heroic inflation of dress gives way to the thrust of fear as the question obtrudes, the fear of disturbing the universe. Which universe? But time can comfort, for it allows the immediate reversal of decisions. So in the element of time Prufrock cheers himself up.

Section IV: lines 49–74] The social theme is resumed, in the element of time. A dislocated pattern of meaningless fragments all echoing back from the impenetrable room. He is within reach of the room, he knows this voice, this order, this universe, but he persuades himself that the courtship would not have been worthwhile after all. How should he, formulated within this social convention, break through it? How can he 'spit out' all the butt ends of his own days and ways? The discarded 'butt-end' carries within itself the sense of burnt-out and discarded days. The balance between line 50 and line 60 is both bitter and apposite. Within these brackets all that he can offer is the single sharp image of pain, the image of a social crucifixion, 'formulated, sprawling on a pin'. Love is as barren as the urban scene, despite the distracting memories of erotic symbols, the arms, the perfume. How then in this familiar world should he begin? The questions propose an inevitable but negative answer. The poem returns to the urban world of the first section, a world now peopled by other lonely men who give to the streets a palpable loneliness that contrasts sharply and movingly with the more subtle loneliness of the social world with which the preceding lines have been concerned. The last five lines of this section are essential to the structure and unity of the poem. They establish the relationship between the streets and the room. The poem is not merely a satire upon a barren social convention; it is about the loneliness and isolation central to human experience; a loneliness given particular poignancy as man reaches towards love. The closing lines reinforce this isolation (lines 73–4), lines that need no apology. They anticipate the sea motif with which the poem is to end. But first, after this interjection, Prufrock returns to the social theme.

Section V: lines 75–110] The cat-like imagery returns as preface to the tea-party, which is to present the moment of decision in love from which Prufrock recoils defeated. He compares himself ironically to John the Baptist and, like him, is betrayed—by his sense of inferiority, and fear of mockery. And so he rationalizes the failure. Would the momentous question have been worth asking, might it not have been greeted with incomprehension or ridicule? What he has known, the streets, the conventional social pattern, and his own place in it, these things cannot easily be set aside, they live in his mind. To proceed would be the worst experience of all, to declare himself publicly, to reveal his flinching nerves to scrutiny and indifference. This is a love poem played out in the mind. All the associations are there; the walk to the loved one, the diffident and uneasy beginning, the agony of how best to bring the matter to an issue, and the ever-present fear of ridicule. But it is not simply concerned with Prufrock: this is how the responses of men have become stultified; this is how they have become what they are.

Section VI: lines 111–31] The end of the poem is prefaced by the Hamlet lines. Hamlet he rejects and assumes rather the rôle of Polonius in deliberate self-mockery, a familiar and necessary defence. But Hamlet is important because, like Faust and Don Quixote, he has become a symbol of Man in Western mythology. He is to bridge the gap between Prufrock and ourselves; the 'You' of the beginning of the poem has been left behind. The line 'Almost, at times, the Fool' leads on to the last deliberately unromantic revolt, the hair parting, the eating of a peach; upon the beach, the sea shore. He can no longer lose himself in the sea as he had earlier wished (lines 73–4). The sea-echoes earlier in the poem are caught up in the mermaids' song, the sound and sight of beauty which Prufrock has heard and seen in imagination, from which he is separated, yet to which he is tied. The sea serves both as image of a creative life and of silence and loneliness; but above all it is the symbol of the inner life with which we cannot communicate effectively in a social world that denies and drowns it. Man, surrounded by a neutral material world, and denied fulfilment in his social world, can take refuge only in this inner world. But when he is recalled from this to reality he there perishes of deprivation and loneliness.

Portrait of a Lady

In this poem, guilt and a sense of inadequacy in human relations attend upon satire and malice. It requires little elucidation, but some account of its movement may be helpful.

The epigraph has been altered from the original by the intrusion of the hesitant dash after 'committed'. What has the young man, a younger relative of Prufrock, committed? Certainly not fornication, yet the pain, the guilt and the uncertainty lurk uneasily behind the malice. This social comedy is played out in three seasons: winter, spring, and autumn. The absence of summer's fulfilment provides its own comment. Note how it catches the essential rhythms of speech which are the precise index of the psychology of the lady; and how Eliot retains a mocking lyric impulse in her word patterns and allows this tone to darken in the final section.

Section I: lines 1–40] This sets the scene and discovers to us the nature of the relationship in both the rhythms and the malicious tone of the verse. This malice is to backfire later. The ironic reference to Juliet's tomb is caught up in the 'resurrection' of Chopin's soul. The pretentious but pitiable conversational gambits of the lady, concealing self-need in artistic patronage, establish a pattern of verbal music that are the rhythms of her personality. Certain keynotes are repeatedly sounded throughout the poem by words like friends, friendship, love, life, feelings, sympathy. They are reinforced by the way in which she seeks to intensify feeling through the hesitant repetition of words and phrases, and by the carefully turned flattery which can become something much more painful and critical:

> '...you knew? you are not blind!
> How keen you are!'

The second paragraph escapes into the secure world of the external and banal as the young man recoils uneasily from an intimacy, the nature of which he does not understand. But the malice of these lines and the dissonance of the musical imagery place him as surely as the lady's music has placed her.

Section II: lines 41–83] Images of revulsion accumulate in this section. The lilac stalk, an image of spring to which reference is soon to be made, with its sad connotation of youth and love, is modified by the twisting of the flower and the reference to the cruelty of youth. The inadequacy of the young man's response offers its own comment. The essential discrepancy between the thing said and the human need it embodies is pointed sharply by the lines that follow, 'My buried life', another echo of Juliet's tomb. His sense of guilt is sharpened poignantly,

> '...how can I make a cowardly amends
> For what she has said to me?'

and painfully as the inadequacy of his responses to the external world are catalogued. The worn-out song and the smell of hyacinths underline the moral dilemma.

Section III: lines 84–124] The time is now autumn and he returns before final departure. George Williamson has noted how Eliot uses a stair image to communicate tension and unease (see 'Prufrock', line 39). The lady's tone is sharp and bitter, despite the despairing echo of her keynotes, 'friends' and 'feelings'. Eliot has used rhyme brilliantly throughout a poem which is in tone essentially naturalistic; it is used, not in a formal scheme, but to reinforce rhythms of voice, to underline irony, and to lend plangency to tones of voice. Above all the rhyme intensifies, as here, the artificiality of a situation which is, nevertheless, challenging and painful. Her final comment has a bitter finality 'I shall sit here, serving tea to friends.' Again the poem moves away at the young man's bidding to the sterile conventions of the external social world before the final paragraph returns to the statement of the epigraph and asks 'What if she should die'? He has withdrawn from a situation which is contrived and false. Yet he had no resources with which to respond to the real problem, the demand for response, affection, help. And had the resources been there, the problem would not have diminished.

Gerontion

All the substantial poems in the volume *Gerontion* (1920) are concerned with the relationship between past and present, with the failure of tradition, and thus look forward to *The Waste Land*. They differ from *The Waste Land*, however, in both their use of the medium of poetry and their tone, which is that of disillusioned despair. They accept and reinforce the isolation, squalor and sterility of the human condition in 1919.

Gerontion has been described by Hugh Kenner as a disembodied sensibility, a voice animating a great silence. It should be added that he is the medium which informs the silence with echoes from a vital past. These echoes deride and judge the present as Gerontion depicts it; the vitality of the poem derives from the negative emotion of despair. Yet the curious anonymity to which Mr Kenner has referred is given life and force by the great rhythmical energy of the poem; a positive and assertive power that contrasts notably with the negative statements that the rhythm largely handles. The opening section, which reinforces the epigraph, will serve as an example. The poem demonstrates the extent to which Eliot had absorbed and understood the function of Jacobean dramatic poetry: not only in his use of the pentameter, but in the unity of mood which characterizes dramatic monologue, imprisoning character and experience in a dislocated sense of reality dominated by verbal images. The image, indeed the verbal structure as a whole, depend upon a use of language that explores the multiple meaning and so set a line echoing with verbal ambiguities which carry the full weight of the linguistic past into the present poetic experience: in brief, the mode of Jacobean poetic drama.

Epigraph] The quotation is from *Measure for Measure*, III. i. The whole of the Duke's speech is relevant, particularly the lines that follow, 'What's yet in this / That bears the name of life?'

1–16] The poem opens with a quotation from A. C. Benson's biography of Edward Fitzgerald which serves to establish themes of helplessness, frenzy and despair as the life-renewing rain is awaited. There is a specific denial of the heroic past (lines 3–6); the images of disintegration that follow underline and establish the complexity of 'the decayed house', a symbol which has a relevance which is not merely personal but cultural. The tremendous rhythmic authority of the lines is important because it asserts the coherence of the abstract intelligence we are to see at work in the poem, the 'dull head among windy spaces', and—at the same time—controls the utterance without losing the sense of desolation and dissolution of values which the poem communicates. Christ was also born at an inn.

17–20] Life-renewing symbols, even rain, are preceded by signs. These lines contain the question put by the Pharisees to Christ and also quote from the great nativity sermon by Lancelot Andrewes, on the union of flesh and logos, to which Eliot refers in his essay on Bishop Andrewes. George Williamson quotes the relevant passage in his *Readers' Guide*. Christ the tiger, the physical incarnation of creative energy, ends this passage and carries us naturally into the next.

21–32] The profligate and dangerous beauty of spring is described in a direct quotation (line 21) from *The Education of Henry Adams*. For Eliot it becomes an image of growth without faith; it is worth noting that the flowers of dogwood are stars, of the chestnut tree candles, and that judas has flowered in more than one sense. The lines that follow deepen the sense of the corruption by the rank growth of spiritual loss and deprivation as Eliot calls in representative figures who are, in Mr Kenner's words 'persons only at the prompting of their names'. Mr Silvero echoes the judas image and the discrepancy of Hakagawa bowing among the Titians is obvious. Madame de Tornquist, whose name suggests the crown of thorns, looks back to the lady of 'Portrait of a Lady' and forward to the spiritualism of Mrs Equitone in *The Waste Land*; finally, the sense of repudiation, loss and guilt is proposed by both the name and posture of the last of these persons.

33–47] This is the heart of the poem. It is both an apology to 'the word' and an explanation of failure in the labyrinth of false clues that we call history, which is truly, so Eliot avers in *Four Quartets*, a pattern ot timeless moments relating man's spiritual to his temporal experience. No such relationship is to be found here. To change the image—and the implication is there (note the echo of Cleopatra)—history is a harlot constantly breeding further invitations to betrayal and disaster, working upon strength to produce weakness and fear, paradoxically enforcing virtue in the face of crime. The verse rhythm and the structure of image and metaphor have great generative power; power which is held in painful tension with what is generated, these tears shaken from the wrath-bearing tree of life.

48–60] Having cast aside faith, made the great refusal, man must abide by the natural order. Time devours. We have reached no conclusion in death about the question posed in line 33: 'what forgiveness?' The echoes from tragedies by Tourneur and Middleton are less important than the deeply moving explanation in which Eliot summarizes the spiritual loss defined in the poem. The vocabulary is, as always, worth close attention; for example, the play on words implied by 'adulterated', the use of the idiom of journalism, which is matched in the following and final section of the poem by the idiom of financial manipulation in the use of words like 'profit', multiply', 'gull', 'Trades'.

61–75] 'These' refer to the senses listed in line 59, impoverished attributes in the situation defined by the poem. The sense of intrigue in the passage on history (lines 33–47), is now transmuted into a bewildering hall of mirrors reflecting the distortions of human endeavour and recalling Mammon in Ben Jonson's *The Alchemist* who desired to multiply variety in a wilderness of mirrors. But the course of nature is not to be interrupted; there follows a sequence of images of destruction which concludes in the image of the gull, the innocent individual, perhaps? Certainly an image of great beauty seen briefly as the drama, which has lived entirely in the words spun from the echoing mind, comes to its exhausted and 'rain-denied' end.

Marina

One of the problems of offering a brief commentary on any of Eliot's mature poems is their relationship with what has gone before. Thus, as 'Prufrock' and 'Portrait of a Lady' identify a society to be more fully treated in *The Waste Land*, so themes both in *The Waste Land*, for example the sea image, and in *Ash Wednesday* are caught up in 'Marina'.

The poem sets two related experiences in tension from the outset: the title points to the regenerative experience of Pericles whose daughter is returned to him as prelude to the return of his wife whom he has committed as dead to the sea; whereas the epigraph from Seneca's *Hercules Furens*, as Hugh Kenner remarks, 'tugs against explicit parallels with Shakespeare's *Pericles* sufficiently hard to arouse a slight but stubborn possibility that the speaker may be mocking himself with falsehood'. The sense of horror as Hercules emerges into the knowledge of his violence is not lost, but is subdued by the wakening and regenerative memory of Pericles as he, in turn, seeks to locate his experience in the physical world apparent to his senses.

The generality of the diction in the poem, the loose but subtly cadenced lyricism, embody an unusual mode of perception in which the eternal is given physical presence and form. Such implications recur in all Eliot's poetry. The poem also conveys the sense both of voyage and voyage ended, which D. E. S. Maxwell relates to Baudelaire's poem 'L'Invitation au voyage'. Certainly, Eliot's essay on Baudelaire should be read in the context of this poem as in others. For example, 'the recognition of the reality of Sin is a New Life', and again, 'the sense of Evil implies the sense of Good'. In 'Marina', the recognition of sin (cruelty, pride, sloth, lust) provides the moral foundation of the poem. The redemption that is proposed is symbolized by images of landscape that may be, as Maxwell suggests, 'transfigured impressions of his youth', namely, the New England coast. The element of transfiguration is clear in the beautiful, slow movement of the old man's perceptions in which the image of his daughter and the fragments of the voyage imagery through which she moves into his conscious mind, mingle the sleeping and the waking world into an apprehension of the eternal and immutable:

'more distant than the stars and nearer than the eye'.

A quotation from 'The Dry Salvages' is apposite:

> '...approach to the meaning restores the experience
> In a different form, beyond any meaning
> We can assign to happiness...'

The approach to the meaning is vital if the poem is to seize upon, make comprehensible, the vision, to remember and dissolve the fog by grace:

> 'I made this, I have forgotten
> And remember.'

The image of the voyage, Pericles' experience, and the theme of rebirth are crucial; they relate not only to the search for vision in the second and fourth books of *Ash Wednesday*, but later to the statement in *Four Quartets*

> 'Old men should be explorers'.

This is not a vague epiphany; it is to see life as a vale of soul-making.

Epigraph] 'What is this place, what region, what part of the world?'
28] *garboard strake:* the first range of planks laid upon a ship's bottom, near the keel.

ISAAC ROSENBERG

Isaac Rosenberg's poetry differs from that of Sassoon and Owen not only technically, but because it springs less directly from disgust or the urgent need to protest by means of satire or by pathos against the war. Rather it seems to find in the war situation an experience that can be grappled into poetry. Certainly the overwhelming experience of trench warfare brings a sharpness of focus into his poetry that is not always found in his earlier writing. Like Owen, he experimented with various poetic techniques and it is probably in his 'Trench Poems' that the command of poetry he had won helped him to achieve his most memorable successes. It is in these poems that the words 'feel after and find' their objective in a personal and impressive way. Though the texture of his writing is deliberately 'rough', exploiting a kind of verbal angularity; and the rhythms are uncompromisingly spare, almost uncomfortably close to those of speech: the poetic structure is so worked that one is always conscious of an energetic interplay between thought and feeling, idea and image. Siegfried Sassoon sums up his achievement:

'Scriptural and sculptural are the epithets I would apply to him. His experiments were a strenuous effort for impassioned expression; his imagination had a sinewy and muscular aliveness; often he saw things in terms of sculpture, but he did not carve or chisel; he modelled words with fierce energy and aspiration...'

Break of Day in the Trenches

1] The druid sacrifice was customarily made as day broke.
2] *It is the same old druid Time as ever:* Time, in the guise of a druid, implacably demands constant sacrifice of the young soldiers' lives. The idea is picked up in lines 14–17 and developed as far as line 22. The 'shrieking

iron and flame' are linked with the rites of sacrifice as well as the bayonets and shellfire of the battlefield. In the same way, line 22 suggests not only the terror of the sacrificial victim but the fear of the soldier when death is imminent.

4] *A queer sardonic rat:* the trench rat, indifferent to either side, *lives*; and by his being alive and his 'detachment' he can afford to see the unlucky soldiers who are killed as victims of a grotesquely sinister joke. The idea implicit in 'sardonic' is developed in 'Droll rat' and 'It seems you inwardly grin'. The ironic mocking tone of lines 7 and 8, and 'Soon, no doubt, if it be your pleasure', confirm this.

23–4] The Flanders poppies grow in the fields where the live soldiers fight and the dead soldiers lie buried ('The torn fields of France'). But the red of poppies' petals is also a metaphor for the blood of the soldiers constantly shed in battle. The poem comes full circle with this metaphor which thus develops the notion of the sacrificial blood of the victim.

25–6] For the moment the poet is safe; he has not been called on to shed his blood—yet. Nevertheless it has been sullied by contact with the searing experience of war.

Returning, We Hear the Larks

1–9] The darkness is instinct with the threat of death. Even the refuge of sleep, back in the camp, is by way of the 'poison-blasted track', the shell-torn and gas-contaminated road which leads to it. But larks' songs, not shells nor shot, 'fall' from the skies. ('Showering' carries with it suggestions of refreshing, cleansing and renewing.)

10–16] The dangerous proximity of death and beauty (the larks' songs) which is the theme of the first three verses, culminates in this verse in three striking similes. The 'dangerous tides' have their counterpart in the danger that is likely to fall from the 'heights of night' in the form of a shell; the girl's beautiful dark hair and her kisses are accompanied by danger too (hence the reference to Eve's serpent and ruin). These similes are also interrelated in so far as both blind man and girl are dreamers, both unaware of danger. The final simile may carry overtones of the Lamia story or the legend of Lilith.

Dead Man's Dump

'Dead Man's Dump' is a distinguished piece of writing. The language never allows the reader to find a refuge from the actuality of the place or the circumstances—the gun carriages that lumber about, near to or over the dead bodies. The apostrophes to the Earth swell out naturally from the disturbing immediacy of the situation.

Title] *Dead Man's Dump:* man is no longer granted the rites of the grave: hence the contemptuous and irreverent 'Dump'. The notion is amplified in lines 61–2.

1] *limbers:* the detachable front of the gun carriage, consisting of two wheels, axle, pole and ammunition box.

1–2] *plunging...Racketed:* Siegfried Sassoon calls Rosenberg 'a poet of movement'. He is so, particularly in this poem, where the insentience and inertness of the dead bodies heightens by contrast the constant movement and noise of the wheels. The reader hears and feels the lurch of '... shattered track / Racketed...'.

3] The simile of the 'crowns of thorns' brings to mind the pain and humiliation and martyrdom of the crucifixion. Owen, in his letters, calls No Man's Land Golgotha—the place of the skull.

4-5] The sceptre, symbol of order and authority, is only partially successful in holding back the 'waves' of cruelty and murder, here seen as fratricide. The sceptres are significantly 'old'. The 'flood' image is used in a changed form later in the poem in lines 59-60, line 68 and line 77.

7] As the poem develops, the wheels of the limbers take upon themselves associations of wheels used long ago in the breaking of criminals. To be broken on the wheel was one of the most painful methods of execution. In the last two stanzas the wheels are at the same time actual and symbolic: the wheels of gun carriages, the wheels as instruments of torture, the wheels of the war machine and the wheels of time and circumstance.

12] Cf. Owen, 'Anthem for Doomed Youth':

> 'The shrill demented choirs of wailing shells'.

30] It is just possible that Rosenberg is utilizing the story of Samson slaying the lion and the bees and honey in its carcass. (Judges v. 5-8). The link is by no means obvious; and, in any case, the image is so adapted that it is subservient to the general line of development in the poem.

32-8] The stanza may carry overtones of the story of Shadrach, Meshach and Abednego (Dan. iv) 'who were cast bound into the midst of the fire':

> 'And the princes, governors and captains and the king's counsellors being gathered together, saw these men upon whose bodies the fire had no power, nor was a hair of their head singed, neither were their coats changed, nor the smell of the fire had passed upon them.' (Dan. iv. 27.)

As with the former image of the bee, the Old Testament story referred to is no more than a kind of palimpsest. A more overt reference to either of these stories would have defeated its purpose; the deployment of ancient stories to give the image a certain amplitude and resonance.

34] *ichor:* ichor was the fluid that flowed in the veins of the gods.

61-2] It is used to be common practice to bury suicides at the crossroads with stakes of holly through their hearts. Gibbets were also placed at the crossroads. The bitter implications are obvious. Rosenberg's mastery of poetic technique makes him pack the maximum implication and suggestion into a phrase. The strength of his poetry lies in the way he works towards realization predominantly through imagery whose cumulative suggestiveness has great power.

WILFRED OWEN

Strange Meeting

The visionary and moral power of this poem make it, in Siegfried Sassoon's words, Owen's 'passport to immortality, and his elegy to the unknown warriors of all nations'.

John Middleton Murry in a review in *The Athenaeum* of the 1920 edition of Owen's *Poems* perceptively commented that the 'verse has a mournful, impressive, even oppressive quality of its own; that the poem has a forged unity, a welded and inexorable massiveness. The emotions with which it is charged cannot be escaped; the meaning of the words and the beat of the sounds have the same indivisible message. The tone is single, low, muffled, subterranean.'

The poem opens in a kind of Dantesque Hell of underground tunnels, at once claustrophobic ('encumbered') and vast ('titanic') where the poet encounters another. (In one draft of the poem, Owen says that the other was 'a German conscript and your friend'; but in the final draft he significantly avoided the specific reference to Germany and decided on the more universal 'I am the enemy you killed'). But the other is as much the poet's other self as the enemy ('And am I not myself' he wrote in one of his letters, 'a conscientious objector with a very seared conscience'). The confrontation leads to the great lament for the loss of youth in war and with it beauty, intelligence and moral purpose; the extinction of the opportunity for human sympathy, generosity and imagination as well as the necessary control of the forces that, uncontrolled, will wreck civilization. Thus the poem becomes a dramatic presentation of Owen's own situation; an elegy for the rich but wasted gift of creativity. In the light of this, the unflinching particularity of the last five lines recalling the final combat, take upon themselves an almost unbearable poignancy.

In this, as in the other poems in this selection, Owen employs pararhyme— a kind of assonantal discord, e.g. 'escaped/scooped', 'groined/groaned'—in order to enhance the sense of unease by denying the reader the satisfaction that comes with a pure rhyme. Pararhyme is Owen's most notable technical innovation.

Anthem for Doomed Youth

Owen uses the ritual associated with the burial of the dead, the passing-bell and the candle, for his own ironic yet compassionate ends.

1] *those who die as cattle:* cf. 'The Send-off', lines 2 and 3.
2–3] The onomatopoeic effect of these lines is strongly marked. The effect is made doubly impressive by the juxtaposition of the booming guns and machine-gun fire with the opening reference to the 'passing-bell'.
9–14] The auditory vividness of the octave gives place to a visual tenderness in the metaphors of the sestet. The silence, the patient resignation in the face of loss, are the more compelling after the diabolic din of the first part of the sonnet.

The Send-off

Owen drafted the poem several times before he finally decided on this form as the most appropriate. The short, almost truncated lines, as if the impulse of vitality has given out in them, convey admirably the overpowering sensation of a doomed expedition. There seems to be room for no more than a numbed compassion in the monosyllabic language and the deliberate uneasiness of the rhythm.

2] *To the siding-shed:* in earlier drafts Owen had written 'to the cattle-shed'. It is curious that the impression remains, in the poem's final form, of the men being herded together like animals in preparation for the abattoir of the battlefield.

4–5] The button-holes and bouquets, symbols of joy and triumph, become, by a macabre, laconic twist in line 5, the flowers used to deck a corpse.

6–10] The only ones who see the departure are the indifferent and the unimportant. Even the signals are seen as momentary accomplices in the criminal 'transportation'.

14–15] The realities of the battlefield; pain, the agony of dying, the indescribable horror, make a travesty of the *idea* of the battlefield in the women's minds.

Exposure

This poem was written in February 1917 and subsequently revised.

The winter of 1916–17 was excessively cold, and conditions in the trenches were almost intolerable. The following extracts from letters written by Wilfred Owen in January 1917 are relevant:

'We are now a long way back, in a ruined village, all huddled together in a farm. We all sleep in the same room where we eat and try to live. My bed is a hammock of rabbit wire stuck up beside a great shell hole in the wall. Snow is deep about, and melts through the gaping roof, on to my blanket. We are wretched beyond my previous imagination—but safe. Last night I had to 'go up' with a party. We got lost in the snow.'...'No Man's Land under snow is like the face of the Moon, chaotic, crater-ridden, uninhabitable, awful, the abode of madness.'...'The people of England needn't hope. They must agitate. But they are not yet agitated even. Let them imagine 50 strong men trembling as with ague for 50 hours!'

And, shortly afterwards, he wrote:

'In this place my platoon had no dug-outs, but had to lie in the snow under the deadly wind. By day it was impossible to stand up, or even crawl about, because we were behind only a little ridge screening us from the Boche's periscope. We had five Tommy's Cookers between the platoon, but they did not suffice to melt the ice in the water-cans. So we suffered cruelly from thirst. The marvel is we did not all die of cold. As a matter of fact, only one of my party actually froze to death'.... 'We were marooned in a frozen desert. There is not a sign of life on the horizon, and a thousand signs of death. Not a blade of grass, not an insect; once or twice a day the shadow of a big hawk scenting carrion...'

The long, drawn-out lines with their exhausted, nerve-worn rhythms; the onomatopoeic exactitude and the melancholy dissonance of the pararhyme work together to communicate with irresistible immediacy the intolerable cold, the sense of isolation ('we were marooned in a frozen desert') and the ghastliness of forced inaction. The recollection of happier times and places, the 'forgotten dreams' of verses 5 and 6 serve by contrast to make more appalling the conditions so disturbingly presented in the earlier verses. The brief escape into memories and dreams breaks up completely in the crystalline nightmare (which is also the reality) of the final verse.

3] *salient:* a rounded projection of the trenches into the enemy line.

13-14] The ironic description of the dawn is remarkable—the clouds at daybreak are seen as sinister battalions of storm troops. The German army wore grey uniforms.

20-5] In a kind of delirium the soldiers dream of a summer countryside.

26-30] The dream shifts to that of an empty house—home.

39] *All their eyes are ice:* Owen's pun is as serious as the 'wit' of the Metaphysicals—and very much more horrifying.

Futility

The tender but uncloying compassion of the first stanza engenders the frustrated protest against the waste of life in the second half of the poem. The sun, universal symbol of life, warmth and growth, is powerless to arouse this sleeper from the snows of death.

9] Owen probably has in mind Gen. ii. 7: 'And the Lord God formed man of the dust of the ground and breathed into his nostrils the breath of life; and man became a living soul.' This memory is perhaps made secular by thoughts of evolution. The sun is seen as source of life.

12] *Was it for this:* death on the battlefield.

   the clay grew tall: the biblical reference works together with the sexual implication to suggest life and growth.

Mental Cases

Cf. 'The Chances', lines 15-18:

> 'But poor young Jim, 'e's livin' an' 'e's not;
> 'E reckoned 'e'd five chances, an' 'e 'ad;
> 'E's wounded, killed and pris'ner, all the lot,
> The bloody lot all rolled in one. Jim's mad.'

In this poem Owen comes closest to the spirit and content of Goya's horrifying 'black' paintings. He spares the reader nothing of the pathos, repulsiveness and terror of insanity brought about by the experience of carnage on the battlefield. The shocked intensity of the poem arises from the concreteness and particularity of the presentation.

26] Imprisoned criminals were once set to 'pick oakum' (to unravel the fibres from which rope is made). These men are like prisoners, but the oakum they pick is for the rope with which they are beaten, in imagination. A knout is a whip, particularly associated with tyranny.

Miners

The poem turns on the extended metaphor of war seen in terms of coal and coalmining with the soldiers as miners who die down in the pit. By means of this exploratory metaphor, Owen works out a series of parallels between the comfortable future, complacently ignorant and indifferent, and the suffering and agony of the present.

1-20] The poet would like to think that the sounds made by the burning coal evoke the world of leaf, fern and elusive animal life of prehistory. Instead the sounds suggest trapped and suffocating miners. (The first hint of this comes in verse 2 explicitly in 'smothered ferns', though the pararhyme carries from the outset a note of menacing echo.) Note the bitter poetic pun in 'wry' and 'writhing'.

21–34] The future enjoys the comfort and ease obtained by the effort (involving suffering, frustration and despair) of the past. In verse eight, Owen unites his themes of mining and war, culminating in the last lines' retrospective pathos.

26] *rooms of amber:* the yellow-orange glow of amber suggests the warmth and light thrown out from the grate. The sound of the metaphor suggests ease and luxury. (Cf. the thin, brusque vowel sounds of the preceding three verses.) The people of the future are immured in their comfortable rooms unaware and not wanting or able to be aware of the processes that have made possible their luxurious existence.

W. H. AUDEN

The Watershed

This early poem is set in the desolate and desecrated landscape that recurs in Auden's later poetry. The maimed landscape serves as a commentary on an historical process, the contemporary condition, and the human situation. Auden, the lonely poetic eye, deftly records the telling detail that points the rape of a countryside, the abandoned workings, the mute despair in the human effort to wring a hard living from the slow and inexorable process of industrial decay. The ramshackle engine and its labours bespeak the effort which is pointed in the effective use of 'grudgingly'. This feeling for landscape and life is reinforced by the illustration Auden chooses, the attempt to clean out the damaged shaft; and its consequences, death by storm, the final resting place reached only through the long-abandoned levels. Against this desolation is set this dour defiance.

The unyielding land offers no content, only frustration, bare and depopulated. Yet the image with which both verse paragraphs end is telling. The poised fox, scenting the danger of man, the predator, echoes the final journey of the dead man who

> 'Through long abandoned levels nosed his way
> And in his final valley went to ground.'

The poem ends with this suggestion of unyielding vitality and life in the natural order, though man seems to echo it only in the fox-like attribute of his death.

In Memory of W. B. Yeats

Each section of the poem is remarkable in itself, the changes of tone and manner no less so.

Section I: lines 1–31] The circumstance and setting of the death opens with a description of almost clinical detachment. Sentiment is given momentary rein in the fourth line before the sombre and moving end of the first stanza. After the contrasts of the second stanza, the natural and the human context briefly placed, the third seizes, through a pattern of finely devised urban imagery, upon the state of the dying man. The fate of becoming one's admirers is pointed, as is the sea-change to which poetry must itself submit; and against the prevailing indifference stand the few who register the sense of loss.

Section II: lines 32–41] Then follows the intensely personal and compassionate address to the dead Yeats and the placing of his poetry, 'A way of happening, a mouth'; like the dying day of the poem's first stanzas, for days like poems miraculously remake themselves.

Section III: lines 42–65] The poem ends with the measured and incisive tread of public celebration, in no sense merely formal, but ending in a moving evaluation of a poet's purpose and achievement.

O What is that Sound

This is one of the most notable and, hence, most familiar of the ballads. The dialogue and the repetitive but ever-changing questions heighten the sense of dramatic tension, wonder, and catastrophe. Fear and horror grow as each successive question receives its quiet and urbane reply. Despite its obvious relationship in form and tone with the medieval ballad, the poem is modern in its chilling implications: it is clearly the product of a period of fear and betrayal when the family sanctities and the images of a continuing and satisfying community existence were shattered as rudely as national boundaries.

On This Island

Richard Hoggart has remarked, in his book on Auden, that this poem is one of a small number of Auden's lyrics given over almost entirely to natural description. He adds: 'Auden's scenery is either a backcloth against which some human situation is considered or a symbol for some activity of the psyche', and quotes:

> 'To me art's subject is the human clay
> And landscape but the backcloth to a torso.'

It is, nevertheless, clear that the 'urgent voluntary errands' of man are introduced in the last stanza to engage and adjust the historical perspective, 'the full view' at which the poem hints. This perspective is introduced in the first stanza when man, the stranger, is enjoined to 'Stand stable here'; an injunction that derives its force from the elements of time and movement both urgent and causal which dictate the rhythm of the poem. The chalk walls oppose the pluck and knock of the tide, yet fall to the foam, and only the containing memory of man provides an element of security. The conjunction of urgent and voluntary in the third line of the last stanza is characteristic. The poem has an ease and fluency which bespeak the great skill of Auden's lyric writing; his power of using, as Hoggart has said, sensuous evocations to reinforce such conceptual epithets as appear in the concluding stanza.

Edward Lear

The transmutation of Edward Lear from 'A dirty landscape-painter who hated his nose' into a land to which children swarmed is handled with a wit which is no less compassionate for being both comic and incisive. This epigrammatic incisiveness is one of Auden's strengths as a poet, deliberately cultivated in his earlier poems to enable him to write conceptually and analytically without losing poetic compression.

Musée des Beaux Arts

Another poem which, like 'On this Island', is concerned with the human condition. Here the form and tone are different, the easy, conversational colloquial speech barely disguise the careful selection and contrast of telling symbol and visual detail of the first paragraph, set as it is against the imaginative recreation of Brueghel's picture, itself an allegory of human aspiration, in the second. Yet, as sometimes happens in Auden's poetry, the poem itself seems almost too accomplished, the reasoning and resolution too easily adjusted to the intellectual occasion.

A Summer Night

Another characteristic poem. The easy flowing lyric line meditates upon the peace deriving from 'this point in time and space' and the gentle security of friendship and contrasts it with the political events of Europe and the impending dangers of the international scene. Repeatedly in Auden's poetry there is this sense of insecurity, the fear of war colouring response to present pleasure of all kinds. An uneasy sense of the difficulty of justifying ease in the face of danger. The transition from the particularity of scene and time and friends is effectively achieved through the image of the cold, remote and indifferent moon. The end of the poem confronts the fate to come and seeks to associate this present moment of calm and grace 'dove-like' with the patience that the impending catastrophe will itself demand. Auden is a master of gentle and colloquial speech which, nevertheless, achieves its own precision and dignity; a precision and dignity sometimes challenged by his use of epithet and image and by the eruption into the quiet and reflective voice of the banal echo of contemporary life. These repay study.

The Unknown Citizen

Mr Hoggart has given a concise and lucid account of the development of Auden's characteristic conversational manner which many of the poems printed in this selection illustrate. In the course of this account, he quotes Auden's comment on Yeats who achieved 'freedom for the most lucid speech with the formal base remaining audible'. Such a manner admits of a great variety of treatments: in this poem, the intention is witty and ironic condemnation of the reduction of the individual to a mere statistic by the processes of modern life. The wit itself makes it difficult to be sure of the seriousness of the intention (Auden's work is too often self-defeating in this was) as reference to chapter XVII of D. H. Lawrence's novel *Women in Love* will sufficiently establish.

INDEX OF FIRST LINES

Indicate the feature of subject matter & style